What people have said about Dr. Auw's previous book *Gentle Roads to Survival:*

"I love Andre Auw's ideas. They contain a great deal of wisdom, wisdom gained from experience."
—Carl Rogers, Ph.D.

"This is one of those rare books that goes to the very heart of life. Simple yet poignant, it speaks to anyone who has ever heard the cry of another human being in pain and wanted to help. It is written for friends, lovers, parents, children, ministers, therapists and partners-for anyone who has ever needed self-healing, or offered solace to another person. A powerful, passionate, enriching book."
—Dawson Church, author of *Facing Death, Finding Love*

"Auw offers a series of suggestions for mastering the 'art of survival' with a gentle and peaceful heart. A follower of the client-centered therapy of Carl Rogers, Auw does not force readers to listen, but rather invites them to find and share their inner beauty and secret hearts. Each chapter reflects on a specific challenge to human existence and is illustrated by anecdotes drawn from Auw's years as a therapist. While some of his ideas appear more geared toward a professional audience, Auw is clearly concerned with individuals and with non-therapeutic relationships; hence his book is in large measure accessible to all."
—Mary Deeley, Booklist Review

"A remarkable book full of wonderful stories and down-to-earth wisdom"
—Helene Hanff

"Want to know how to help someone in pain?....read this book! If I ever needed to seek mental help, Dr. Auw is the kind of psychologist I would want to see."
—...Review

ASLAN PUBLISHING—OUR MISSION

Aslan Publishing offers readers a window to the soul via well-crafted and practical self-help books, inspirational books and modern day parables. Our mission is to publish books that uplift the mind, body and spirit.

Living one's spirituality in business, relationships, and personal growth is the underlying purpose of our publishing company, and the meaning behind our name Aslan Publishing. We see the word "Aslan" as a metaphor for living spiritually in a physical world.

Aslan means "lion" in several Middle Eastern languages. The most famous "Aslan" is a lion in *The Chronicles of Narnia* by C. S. Lewis. In these stories, Aslan is the Messiah, the One who appears at critical points in the story in order to point human beings in the right direction. Aslan doesn't preach, he acts. His actions are an inherent expression of who he is.

We hope to point the way toward joyful, satisfying and healthy relationships with oneself and with others. Our goal is to make a real difference in the everyday lives of our readers

Barbara & Harold Levine Publishers

The Gift of Wounding

Finding Hope & Heart in Challenging Circumstances

Andre Auw, Ph. D.

Aslan Publising
Fairfield, Connecticut

Published by
Aslan Publishing
2490 Black Rock Turnpike #342
Fairfield, Connecticut 06432

For a free catalog of our complete line of titles or
to order more copies of this book call (800) 786-5427.
Visit our web site at www.aslanpublishing.com

Library of Congress Cataloging-in-Publication Data:
Auw, Andre, 1923-
The gift of wounding : finding hope & heart in challenging circumstances / Andre Auw. — 1st ed.
p. cm.
Includes bibliographical references.
ISBN 0-944031-79-X
1. Life change events—Psychological aspects. 2. Change (Psychology) I. Title.
BF637.L53A98 1999
158.1—dc21 98-30152
CIP

Cover design by Linda Hauck
Interior design by Brenda Plowman
Printed in Canada
First Edition

10 9 8 7 6 5 4 3 2 1

Table of Contents

Acknowledgements

My deepest thanks to Judy Tompkins for her initial work on the manuscript, to Brenda Plowman for her artistic work on this and my previous book, to Marcia Yudkin for her splendid editing, and finally to Barbara and Hal Levine, who have encouraged and supported me through the final stages of publication.

Foreword

If our entire world were collapsing around us, we would want to have Dr. Andre Auw as our therapist. His words of healing and hope are timely and educational for therapists and clients alike. We believe anyone suffering adversities or having a professional interest in psychotherapy can gain valuable knowledge from this book. We have made his previous book, *Gentle Roads to Survival: Making Self-Healing Choices in Difficult Circumstances,* required reading in our clinic, as we will with this new book.

In an age of behavioral approaches to therapy, Dr. Auw comes as a breath of fresh air. Instead of treatment plans he offers hope, healing and love. He has a profound faith in the ability of people to direct their own lives. Everyone from student to client to psychotherapist can benefit from the wise writings of this extraordinary man. He offers a rare insight into the Person-Centered Approach of his former colleague, Dr. Carl Rogers.

More than merely a teacher or psychologist, Dr. Auw is the kind of person you would love to have as a neighbor living next door. You would invite him over for dinner often. Very often indeed.

–Laurie A. Grengs M.A.L.P., President
–Jim McCaffrey, Director,
Associated Counseling Clinic,
Fridley, Minnesota

Introduction

The journey along the road to survival is marked by a number of intersections where we must make a choice. In this book, I have suggested ways in which we can make better selections for ourselves. There is no single path that represents the perfect path for us, and we can always retrace our steps and choose a different route. Growth consists in learning from our mistakes, as well as being open to taking new risks.

When we choose well, the path enables us to travel with more confidence and inner feelings of security. Fear lessens and our sense of well-being increases.

One of the sources of reassurance for our journey is the fact that others have travelled along these roads before us. I have included some of their stories and reflections as a form of guidance and inspiration for us when the travel becomes difficult.

These stories remind us that our healing and growth must begin in the heart, as must our choices of paths to follow. It is when our hearts are touched that our vision expands, new options and hope emerge, and better life choices become possible.

May you find in these pages some of that inspiration and vision. If this is true, then I in turn will feel gifted and blessed.

– Andre Auw, Ph.D
Honolulu, Hawaii

CHAPTER ONE

An Invitation to Newness

Albert Schweitzer's goal as a young man was to be a good minister. But after a period of studying theology, he found himself questioning many interpretations of scripture and came to an important decision. He said later,

> *"I developed some ideas of my own which were at variance with the ideas that had been taught me...I decided I would leave the seminary. Instead of trying to get acceptance for my ideas, involving painful controversy, I decided I would make my life an argument...I would attempt to have my life and work say what I believed."*

This was a dramatic moment for Schweitzer; it was an invitation to newness that ultimately took him to his career as a healing physician in the primitive village of Lambarene, Africa.

I believe that many of us receive a number of invitations to newness in our lives. Some are equally dramatic, others less so, but they are important opportunities and challenges to move in new directions. Sometimes, because of the various distractions and the stress of our lives, we may not even recognize the inner promptings that suggest new possibilities. At other times, we may hear the invitation and reject it out of our fear of the unknown. It may be helpful to reflect upon some of those lost opportunities in order to see a pattern in our response to newness.

As in the example of Schweitzer, some of our invitations will come out of frustration and disappointment. The road we have been traveling may begin to feel either like a dead-end or a detour. Feelings of general dissatisfaction can be a prelude to moving in a new direction. At other times the invitation may appear in the form of a sudden burst of awareness that some change is needed in our lives. Also, the invitation may come by way of what seems an "accidental" offer or request by another person.

This latter possibility occurred in my own life. I was invited to co-teach a course for a graduate summer program. I had not taught before and felt somewhat inadequate, but the prospect of sharing the teaching made it less frightening. At the last moment my colleague said that another commitment had arisen and thus he would be unable to join me. I was "on my own," with feelings of panic. However, I summoned up my courage and rushed to prepare twice the material and taught the course.

Despite a rather shaky beginning, I felt the support of the students and had a very rewarding experience. This was, indeed, an invitation to newness for me, and the beginning of a new aspect of my lifework. Since that first course I have taught in colleges and universities around the world, bringing to me new experiences with different cultures and peoples. I am constantly grateful for the invitation that has so abundantly enriched my life.

A colleague of mine received his call to newness from a sudden insight that his life was incomplete. He said,

> *"One day I was watching a beautiful sunset by the seashore, and I felt a kind of inner pang. I realized that although I had accomplished many of my goals, my life was basically selfish. I felt that I was called to something greater. My awareness of this lack led me to volunteer for the Peace Corps, in which I served for several years. It was a life of hardship and sacrifice, but I have never been happier in my life than in helping people to learn better survival skills."*

Today he and his wife regularly work as volunteers in a community health clinic and see this as part of their mission in life.

Responding to life's invitation to new challenges is never a simple or easy choice. We are faced with many unknown obstacles and all our ancient fears rise to deter us from choosing to take the risk. Most of us resist change when it is first presented to us. We like to be comfortable, even with what has become a rut for us. We are very reluctant to venture forth in a new direction when it appears to be moving along a dark path and heading into a forest.

Yet it is also true that life itself is characterized by change. Philosophers have compared it to a river that is always flowing, changing directions and pace, finding new ways to continue its course to the sea. Fear of change can be lessened when we remind ourselves of this reality. We cannot escape change; it makes sense to find better ways to respond to it.

Plato reminds us that our fears become like sailors on a ship who, fearful of the unknown voyage ahead and unhappy with conditions aboard, threaten mutiny. As captain of the ship, we must take charge and quell the mutiny.

Refusing to take a particular risk will not in itself assure us a safe journey. Life will continue to present challenges through its ongoing changes, affecting our physical and emotional health as well as our relationships. One remedy is to listen more sensitively to our hearts when the invitation appears. It is a very reliable guide to choices that are necessary for us. The heart will indicate when it is time to "seize the moment."

I remember a graduate student, who was in the Navy, telling me that he had what he termed "a wake-up call." He had been planning on a business career, but his work with Little League baseball showed him how much good could be accomplished with young boys who had a strong male role model. At the same time, he felt that the long years of training that it took to become a counselor made that an impossible dream. However, he began to take different workshops and short courses. By the time he left the Navy he was ready to begin working in a clinic, where he not only served as a counselor, but coached young boys in baseball and basketball.

His impossible dream became a reality, partly because he found a way to move forward despite his fears. He realized his dream in segments. The risks for these were small and manageable. And over several years he was able to build his skills and his confidence. His work with boys has gained him honors, as well as the gratitude of countless young men and the community at large.

There is a special kind of challenge that comes to men and women after a failed marriage or the death of a spouse. When the invitation to newness comes in the form of a serious attraction to someone, there is an overriding fear that expresses itself in the form of a question. An inner voice, full of doubt asks, "Can I begin again? Do I want to?" And as long as we frame the question in those terms, we will most likely be unable to respond positively to the invitation. We get locked into our memory of past problems, failures, and guilt over past behavior. We cannot hear the wisdom of the heart because we are making too much noise with our inner fear-filled chatter.

For this situation we need first to be nourished with beauty: a glorious dawn sky filled with blueness and clouds, a few moments in a shaded wood, or by a secluded lake or stream. We need to drink in the beauty, without thinking or inner conversation. There must be some stillness to soften the heart and quiet the mind, and heal the soul. Then perhaps we can hear the heart and be guided by its wisdom.

One of my clients discovered the impact of this approach. She spent a few days at a small cabin in the mountains. She took long walks in the forest, listened to bird songs, smelled the fragrance of pine trees, and dipped her feet in an icy stream. She resolutely refused to allow her fears to intrude. She told me that she spoke to her inner fears and said, "I am going to deal with your concerns after this weekend, but not now. So shut up!" And they did. When she returned home, she knew as soon as she walked through the front door that her heart had spoken and that she was ready to accept the invitation to risk a new relationship. It has proven to be a wise and rewarding choice.

I think it is important to realize that these invitations are not preceded by trumpet blares or messages written in the heavens for all to see. They are gentle inner voices, soft but insistent pulsings of the heart, difficult to hear unless we are trained to listen for them, but powerful by their consistency and conviction. That is why one of the best things we can do for ourselves is to prepare for the reception of these invitations.

Learning to listen to the beauty of nature, to be touched by the suffering of others, to reach out with compassion to those in need—these are the keys that open our hearts and permit us to hear messages that would otherwise be missed by the busy noise of our everyday existence.

A journalist who visited Mother Teresa in Calcutta said that the love and genuine compassion of the nuns and helpers prompted an awareness of the shallowness of her life. When she returned to New York, she volunteered for work with an AIDS clinic and later said,

> *"It was not some heroic gesture. I simply felt a need to reach out to others in some small way, and I feel that I receive back much more than I give."*

The invitation to newness need not be life-altering experience or transformation. It can be something as simple as an offer to view things in a new way or to experience people and situations differently. I recall a woman in her fifties who said that she had lived a rather sheltered life, and had never been exposed to the world of music or fine art. At the invitation of a friend she went to a lecture on Impressionist artists. She said, "At first I thought the art was terrible. Why couldn't the artists paint a picture that was clear for people to see? My limited experience with art had been traditional representational art: plates of fruit, Madonnas with child, that sort of thing."

But the lecturer helped her to "look into" the painting and then view it with a different kind of vision. The woman found herself fascinated by the skill of the artist and she said, "I became entranced with the works of Monet and Rouault, marveling at the power of their works to touch my heart." Her response to this invitation to newness led to a lifelong love affair with Impressionist paintings, taking her to the great museums of Europe and filling her final years with a great source of nourishment and delight.

The invitation to simple new directions such as these may appear as an offer to try something different: a lecture, a concert, a visit to a museum, even things as prosaic as a change in dress, or a new way of preparing food.

A friend of mine wrote a cookbook in which she encouraged the reader to experiment with her recipes, using them simply as a basic foundation. She called it the *Try It Cookbook.* And her intention was to encourage the reader to imagine other ingredients or ways to prepare a dish. Beginning cooks loved the book and found the courage to experiment with small changes at first, and then with greater boldness as they saw the success of their experiments.

The willingness to take one of these small risks can become an alteration of our basic attitude toward change with even more significant impact on our lives. The fear associated with newness and the unknown is considerably diminished by these small risks taken over a period of time.

The invitation to newness is in essence an offer to view reality in a new way. It is this different way of looking at things that is an introduction to scientific discovery. The scientist has learned the value of Chesterton's famous remark, "We should look at familiar things until they appear strange."

Albert Einstein had this experience when one day he questioned the familiar way of viewing the composition of matter. His 'strange' way of looking at it saw a new relationship to energy, and thus his famous formula which revolutionized the understanding of the physical world.

The readiness to see things in a new light can affect not only the way we view the world around us, but also our attitudes, our prejudices, our values and our relationships. For years spiritual masters have encouraged retreats and vacations where we have greater contact with nature and more opportunity for solitude. The soul gets nourished, the heart is quieted, and the mind can permit itself to view one's life from a different perspective.

❀

There are always risks with change, but there are always risks in each aspect of our lives. It seems to me that the invitation to newness proposes not so much a dangerous journey into a frightening place, as an exciting adventure into a new world. It is less an entry into an arena of lions, and more a journey to the moon.

The heart says, "take the adventure." I like the attitude of a modern dancer who says he has adopted this motto towards newness: **"If it ain't risky, don't do it."**

CHAPTER TWO

Looking Toward the Horizon

From my window I can choose to look down and see the traffic moving alongside of the canal, or I can look out past the golf course towards the houses clinging to the flanks of the hills. Or I have a third choice. I can lift my eyes above the hills to the cloud-filled sky and from there to the distant horizon. Whenever I choose this latter view I experience something more than mere observation. I feel an inner quiet and a need to remain for a moment in a state of reflection.

This latter choice gives me not only information from the world outside, it also makes a connection with my inner self. It is as if my heart has been touched, or my soul affected, by this experience. I believe this added dimension transforms a visual experience into a revelation and, at times, even a kind of epiphany.

I find many applications of this way of viewing reality in everyday living. As problems arise our immediate reaction is to look down, to focus our attention and energy on the problem itself. And even though we think we are searching for a solution, our creative energy remains dormant because our inner vision is locked into a problem-focus.

Looking down, in addition, most often is characterized by a negative atmosphere of fear which confuses and even paralyzes our mental processes. The result is an inner feeling of helplessness, a sense of "I can't." At such a moment some kind of distraction can alter our negative focus, and permit us to look beyond the pain or the problem.

Recently the singer Tony Bennett described the way in which singing could accomplish this for him. A painful migraine would seem to vanish once he was absorbed in the lyrics of a song he loved.

An even more effective way to move out of the looking-down focus is to experience the power of shared love. The heart touched by love enables us to glimpse a wider environment and additional options. It allows us to look beyond these limited possibilities to a horizon of hope and belief in ourselves, which fuels our abilities to make new choices for the future.

I remember seeing this happen in an encounter group. A nun had described her feelings of sadness at not having the rewards of teaching any more. She had retired from teaching because of her age. She judged herself to be too old to be effective with young students. However, a young man in the group said to her, "Sister, I think you are being too hard on yourself. Maybe high school students are not for you. But I have been impressed with your insights and ability to communicate with this mixed group and I think you would be a fantastic teacher for college students. I personally would love to learn from you."

Because his words were sincere and from the heart, the nun could accept and embrace them as true for her. In that brief exchange, her inner focus moved from looking down at her life situation to looking out toward a new horizon of possibilities. Later I heard that she had accepted a position in a college and was both successful and delighted with the experience. She described her new life in a few words, "I feel as if I have come home, and it's wonderful." Such an apparently small gift, yet it had a profound impact on her life.

A downward focus can arise not only from an assessment of our ability, but also from a fear of "launching into the deep" by ourselves. Change of focus can be best aided by a sense of strong loving support. Parents, teachers, and coaches often offer this support. For the fearful and hesitant person, this supportive attitude suggests, "I believe you can do it with a bit of extra help."

Fear shared is often fear banished. Mutual support allows us to replace paralyzing fear with hope. We can look to the distant horizon and feel encouraged rather than dismayed.

Maria Montessori was able to help children change their negative focus in remarkable ways. Her loving manner encouraged the children by making learning an enjoyable series of shared discoveries. A story is told of her school children receiving a gift of cookies, and their delight in the various shapes of the cookies: "Look! Here is a rectangle!" And, "Oh, I have a triangle and a square!" The enjoyment of eating the cookies was no less than the joy of uncovering a new learning.

Montessori was preparing the children for life by awakening in them a sense of inner power, the ability to learn new things and find solutions to problems. Love, sharing, and having fun while learning were her ways of seeing the horizon filled with hope, rather than fear and dread.

An inner sensing or intuitive insight can also move us from a negative focus to a more positive outlook.

A young woman in a London sanitarium experienced such a change. Hospitalized for tuberculosis she seemed to be getting weaker after her regimen of a bland diet, no hot baths, and complete bed rest. An inner voice said, "Take a nice, long hot bath." She did, and felt much better. Next, she asked her friends to bring her some of her favorite foods, which she ate and enjoyed.

When her doctor discovered this he scolded her saying, "You can't do these things. You have to follow my instructions." The young woman, emboldened by her experiments said to the doctor,

> *"Doctor, you seem to be laboring under the assumption that I am working for you. Actually, you are being hired to care for me. I will follow your instructions as long as they appear to be helping me to get well. But I have discovered that my body knows what is best for its health, and I intend to follow its instructions as a priority. Now, if you can accept that, I think we can work together to get me well."*

The doctor, somewhat reluctantly, agreed and within a few months her lungs were clear and she was discharged. That original intuitive insight enabled her to move from feelings of discouragement and fear to an inner sense of hope as she looked to the future.

These are some of the experiences that can prompt a change in focus: a distraction, the presence of loving support, the discovery of a newly acquired skill or learning, and trusting the voice of intuition. By responding to one of these experiences, we will find that our fixation with a negative focus is broken and we are free to look beyond the concern with the problem facing us, and search for the promise inherent in the horizon of the future.

The operative word here is "experiences." Ideas, concepts, and words seldom, of themselves, are effective in changing focus. We need to sense or feel some inner compulsion to act rather than think about, to do rather than discuss.

Only an experience which touches the heart has power to stir us into action. The emotional impulse may be negative like anger or fear, or it may be positive like joy or feeling loved, but such inner sensings are the prelude to an act of will that alters the way we view a current life situation.

Choosing to look beyond the challenge or crisis of the moment brings new vistas, different colors and patterns, and most important, new possibilities. This in turn becomes the seedbed for a new experience of hope and self-confidence.

In recent years the concept of holistic health, recognizing the unity of mind, body and spirit within an individual, has given us more tools to use in our pursuit of health. One of these celebrates the importance of experience. Often various experiential exercises will result in an awareness that at times can be transformational.

I recall a woman in a workshop who had been stuck in her resentment toward her husband, from whom she was currently separated. She had discussed her feelings in a number of therapy sessions without success.

The group facilitator asked her if she would be willing to try an exercise, and she agreed. He instructed her to repeat a few words over and over, without attending to the meaning. He asked her to say: "Joe, I love you." When she started to protest, he gently reminded her not to think about the meaning but simply to say the words.

He had her say the words loudly, softly, and gently, with differing tones. Gradually her voice changed and the words sounded like a caress. She was then asked to repeat the following words, "Joe, I hate you." The words were flat at first, and as she increased her volume they became stronger expressions of anger, and then a remarkable thing happened. Having experienced her anger as she heard her voice saying the words, she stopped suddenly, and breaking into tears she cried out, "No, I don't hate you. I love you, I love you."

Only when she experienced her mixture of inner feelings could she uncover her true caring for her husband. She later expressed astonishment that such a simple exercise could have been so liberating for her.

Today most counselors understand the value of experience in enabling clients to move out of a fixation with their current pain or problem.

I have found that even in the midst of serious examination of their concerns, it can be most helpful to suggest some physical exercise. A short period of deep breathing, or a gentle stretching of the arms and legs, can bring us back to the issue with a slightly different feeling. And the experience of visualization or role playing, because they involve the body and the imagination, can have a powerful effect in fostering a change of focus and attitude. These are tools that can move us out of simply thinking about our problems and into feeling empowered to do something about them.

Carl Rogers, the renowned psychologist, told of a schizophrenic client who participated in a group therapy session which he facilitated. The man sat through numerous sessions for several weeks without saying a word. At the final session he announced, "I want to say something." The group members waited eagerly for his first contribution. His brief remark summarized the impact of his group experience. He said, "Because of these sessions I can say that I don't know what I am going to do in the future, but I know I'm going to do it."

Somehow, this silent man had internalized a feeling of self-confidence that impelled him to want to take charge of his life. His focus moved from the negative sense of helplessness to a vision of hope that filled him with excitement as he looked toward the horizon.

His words can serve as a source of inspiration for us:

"I don't know what I'm going to do, but I know I'm going to do it."

CHAPTER THREE

Eliminating the Static

When any dramatic event occurs in life, we find ourselves facing an uncertain future with concern and anxiety. Our fears may be based on past experience, and may seem quite justified. Unfortunately the manner in which we frame the question in our minds, as we think of the future, may serve to increase our fears and impede our progress rather than provide us with new options.

"What else?" can be a statement of angry frustration: "What ELSE can happen?" It can also be a confession of helplessness: "I have no idea of what I can do next." Or it can be a declaration of impotence: "I have no marketable skills, and I am too old to find a new job." Asking that basic question of ourselves can most often be an exercise in negative thinking which leads to feelings of hopelessness and depression. However, being aware of the type of question we are asking can enable us to re-phrase our question of concern. This will reflect more positive feelings and elicit more practical responses to our dilemma.

In the New Testament, there is a story of a steward fired by his master which illustrates this point. His first question was framed by his fear and filled with negative possibilities. "What am I to do? To dig I am not able, and to beg I am ashamed." Then he became aware of his attitude and an "Aha!" came to him. "I know what I will do. I will contact my master's creditors, etc." The details of his plan are less important than the fact that he emerged from what could have been a mental paralysis and feelings of desperation and depression.

Becoming aware of our internal conversation can lift us out of the sticky marsh of feeling victimized and onto a path of new options. "Why" questions soon reveal the fact that we are stuck in the problem, as well as burdened by the weight of self-pity: "Why me?" translates easily into, "Poor me!" It is wiser to immediately examine our initial reaction to a demanding challenge or a crucial decision. We may be able to short-circuit the usual process of self-doubt and self-pity.

A woman during an encounter group session spoke of her sadness and sense of loss. She had been married to a wealthy man who left her for a younger woman. And when she lost her lovely home and moved into a tiny apartment, she discovered that she had also lost her friends. No one called or came to see her. She felt abandoned and betrayed. It was also apparent that she saw herself as a victim.

After some moments another woman responded to her.

> *"Joyce, when you were describing your situation it was like déjà-vu for me. I went through a similar experience a few years ago. I felt completely lost, and also ashamed and humiliated because I had to go on welfare. My mother helped me to get out of that depression. She told me that all these people who abandoned me were not my friends at all.*

"She said, 'They were simply non-paying customers who attended the parties and dinners you gave. In a way, you needed them to have a party and they helped to make the parties a success. But they were like theater-goers who got free tickets to a performance. They came, enjoyed the performance, applauded, and then went their way. Your mistake was in believing that they really cared about you. Nonsense! They served their purpose. Now forget them and create a new life with a few real friends.'

"It was a true revelation for me. That very day I began to see myself and my future in a new light, and I am much more independent and happy."

Her words were not lost on Joyce. She said, "Thank you so much for sharing that experience with me. I needed your story to pull me out of my self-pity. I hope I can stay in touch with you for support from time to time." And that is what happened. Six months later the two women started a small boutique which is now making good profits. But they both admit that the best part of the business is the way they can support each other with caring and humor.

Sometimes we may be jolted out of our negative thinking by an external event. A friend told of this happening to her. An automobile accident took place just outside her home. Running to the scene, she saw that a woman in the passenger seat was dazed and bleeding from a head wound. She dashed into the house, got a pitcher of water, cloths and a basin, and a glass. She gently bathed the woman's face, cleansed the surface wound, offered her a drink of water and comforted her until an ambulance arrived.

The injured woman sent her a bouquet of flowers a few weeks later along with a note of gratitude saying,

> *"You will never know how much your caring gesture meant to me. I was terribly frightened, and your comforting presence made me feel assured that I would be all right."*

In recalling this incident, my friend said,

> *"That afternoon I was sitting in my living room. I was feeling very lonely, missing my children who were away at school, and concerned about my health at mid-life. The accident took me out of my obsession with myself. I was needed, and there were things I could do to help another human being. I decided to volunteer at a nearby hospital, and my life has taken on new meaning. It is so rewarding to offer small gifts of love to people who are ill and in pain. I have not only made many new friends, but I feel that I am giving back something to life. I have never felt so rich and full."*

It is a truth as ancient as it is precious, that in going out of our way to help others we find our own needs being met.

A colleague who characterized himself as "a consistent worrier" described a change in attitude that occurred after reading a magazine article. He said,

> *"The writer referred to 'inner static,' as a description of the running monologue that our mind carries on all the time. He said that very often our self-talk is negative and colored by fear and anxiety. The static blocks out positive thoughts and feelings, and actually increases our fearfulness. His remedy was: STOP AND LISTEN! He also added that* ***when we hear ourselves asking questions like, 'Why do I?,'***

'Why can't I,' and 'Will it ever change?,' we can be sure we are sabotaging ourselves."

My friend discovered, as he reflected on his own inner musings that they were filled with similar questions. Now, when he can hear that kind of negative thinking he says to himself, "I refuse to continue such thoughts. I will open my mind to thoughts and feelings of gratitude for being alive and healthy, and for being gifted enough to meet any future challenges." This newfound ability to direct his inner thoughts has not only lifted him out of his former self-doubts, it has enabled him to release his creativity, and has brought him a more peaceful inner spirit.

Insight into our inner patterns of self-talk can also be aided by disclosing our thoughts and feelings to a trusted friend or counselor. If this person is able to listen and reflect what is heard rather than offer advice, we may be able to hear the anxiety behind our inner questions. A therapist said that one of her clients was astonished to discover that she also visited a therapist from time to time. The client said, "Why would you have to go to a therapist?" And she received this reply, "I'll tell you why. Because I need to hear what I am saying to myself, and sometimes I can't hear it by myself." I find this a good motto for all of us to treasure.

Similar mottoes, adages or aphorisms have been used by saints and wise teachers throughout the ages. The expressions can be of a religious nature, as one of the psalms, "the Lord is my shepherd," a poetic phrase, or reminders of the beauty that surrounds us. In the latter case, a Buddhist monk said that his master gave him a recipe for restoring the inner peace that sometimes eluded him because of his tendency toward sudden anger. Rather than suggesting he try to overcome his anger, the master said to him,

> *"Search for beauty when you first awaken, and let it be your last thoughts before you sleep at night, and you will discover a wonderful treasure."*

The monk said that for over forty years he had used that motto and had discovered beauty, not only in nature, but also in the monks and people he met during the day.

Beauty has always been a source of "lifting our hearts and minds" above the trials and concerns of daily life. In my own experience I have been fortunate to have traveled to many different countries. In each place that I have visited, I have received gifts of beauty that I shall treasure forever. These have been moments of transcendence that touched my soul deeply.

I recall one evening at sunset on a mountaintop in Japan. From that one vantage point I could see seven different mountain ranges. It had just stopped raining. The sun breaking through the clouds filled the different peaks with colors of rose and purple, misty greys against the dark green flanks of the lower hills. I stayed for several minutes, transfixed by the stunning beauty and feeling at one with this wondrous gift of creation.

I have had other soul-stirring experiences while gazing at the majesty of the cliffs of Moher in Ireland, and the windswept heather-clad Isle of Skye in Scotland. I was gifted with the sight of daffodils growing wild in the Lake District of England, the very spot where long ago Wordsworth penned his famous lines honoring this lovely flower. And recently I had the joy of experiencing the incredible golden light that suffuses the entire countryside in the hills above Nice and in the corners of Provence. Time seems to stand still and offers an invitation to be filled with this beauty and, even for a few moments, to rise above the concerns of daily life and the fears for the future.

Whatever method we choose to lift ourselves above the rut of negative thoughts and feelings, from trying to hear our inner conversations, to disclosing these to another person, to finding insight through reading or to discovering an adage or aphorism that speaks to us, or finally, to engage in a search for beauty, will bring certain rewards to us.

The words of the master to his student monk can also be directed to us: **"Search for beauty and you will discover a wonderful treasure."**

CHAPTER FOUR

The Gift of Wounding

Several years ago I read a remarkable book by Henri Nouwen, entitled *The Wounded Healer*. I was touched by the way in which the author was able to view his personal suffering as a gift. He said that his own pain had made him more compassionate and understanding of the suffering of others.

The concept made sense to me intellectually, but it was not until some years later that I experienced it as a reality in my own life.

In counseling a man whose wife had been killed in an auto accident, I found myself recalling my own pain and anger over the recent death of my sister under similar circumstances. I could feel this man's pain in my own heart, and was able to allow him to experience his conflicting emotions and express them. We developed a bond of closeness, becoming like companions on a difficult journey, rather than patient-with-a-problem and doctor-with-the-answer.

Gradually, this man was able to ride out the suffering and grief, and to move from feelings of self-blame to putting his energy into building a new life. Later he wrote, telling me of the peace he felt in his heart about the death of his wife, and the positive change in his outlook. He added also that his painful experience had helped him to become a kind of companion to a colleague who had lost her husband. He said, "I now see that the death of my wife, so difficult for me to accept, proved to be a hidden blessing, for I could understand and help someone else who was grieving."

This experience enabled me to internalize the concept of spiritual and emotional wounding as a gift. At the same time I recognized that being able to view suffering in this manner takes time, and usually the loving support of someone whose compassion is based on personal experience. We often need that kind of inspiration and guidance as we struggle with our impatience to be healed. And yet it is also true that our pain can be eased and our perception altered by a variety of experiences.

One of the terrible side effects of suffering is a seeming inability to focus upon anything but the pain. We think about it constantly and allow our minds to obsess on the whys and hows associated with our suffering. It is as if we have been hypnotized by our anguish. At such times it may be best to allow ourselves to feel the pain and flow with it, rather than denying it or attempting to deaden it by drugs or alcohol. If we are able to do this, we may come to a point where we can begin to see the value of this suffering in our lives.

Saints and mystics can teach us how to do this. They have learned that suffering is a part of the fabric of our life experience. It is not a rare tragedy that occasionally befalls us. From the beginnings of the birth process to the final moments before death, pain is an essential part of that process. Each stage of our growth through adolescence and adulthood is marked by painful interior struggles.

Holy men and women understand and accept this. As a result they can more easily integrate suffering into their lives as it appears. They are also sensitive to the personal message that is conveyed by a particular trial or pain. They can even embrace it as a friend who, out of love, offers an opportunity for growth. And they believe they have power over the impact of pain in their lives.

It may seem that this understanding of pain is only for saints and mystics, and not for ordinary people like ourselves. But the fact is that we already possess a portion of their understanding which we demonstrate in many ways. At the onset of a headache we run to the medicine cabinet for a pill. We believe the pill will lessen the pain or banish it completely. We are aware that anesthetics can enable us to endure surgery without pain. Similarly we may have had experience with acupuncture or hypnosis as other means of dealing with pain.

These examples remind us that our brains can intercept the messages of pain, if we can access those parts of the brain-functions. We may also recall stories of athletes severely injured, yet so focused upon finishing their event, that they did not feel pain until the event was completed.

Thus, we are already aware of the power of the mind to affect the experience of pain. Not only can we reduce pain, but we have a similar ability to intensify the experience of physical and emotional suffering by the way in which we obsess upon our wounding. We think about it, and feel anger because of it. Like Job in the Old Testament, we may rail against God and seek to assign blame for our hurt.

It is our choice whether we use our minds to increase our suffering or mitigate it. But at times we may need some assistance in shifting our perception.

A friend, Dr. Mitsuo Aoki, now retired as Dean of the Department of Religion at the University of Hawaii, is also a minister who now spends many hours visiting seriously ill men and women. Aware of their fear of dying and their concern with physical pain, he often uses a simple demonstration to illustrate a point he wants them to consider. Holding a pen before them he will say, "Tell me what you see." The person will most often say, "A pen." Dr. Aoki will nod and then ask, "And what else do you see? Gradually, like Socrates using his Maieutic Method, he elicits answers such as these: "I see your body, the color of your shirt, the window behind you, and the curtains blowing in the wind. I see the painting hanging on the wall and the flowers on the dresser."

The responses indicate a significant change in focus and perception, from a narrow locked-in frame of reference to the larger frame of the whole environment surrounding the central object. Dr. Aoki explains that when people hear a diagnosis such as "cancer," they tend to think "terminal" and remain locked into that fear-filled perception.

But if they become aware of the broader perspective of their lives as the environment in which cancer is simply a part, they can begin to stimulate their immune systems and activate their healing energies. Their focus is on living fully until they die, rather than slowly dying, however short or long that time may be.

This change in perception can be triggered in many ways, some of them by unusual events or incidents. A client shared a radical change in the way he viewed his own physical and emotional suffering. For several months he had been lost in feelings of self-pity after losing his job due to ill health. Then a remarkable thing happened. He described it in a letter to me.

> *"One beautiful sunny morning I was taking my usual walk, feeling quite sorry for myself, when I noticed an old friend coming down the street toward me. I had not seen him for several months and missed him. He was a small black and white fox terrier who had always seemed full of life, wagging his tail as he stopped to let me pet him. But this day I was aware that something was wrong. He was running in a rather lop-sided manner, leaning to his right. I soon discovered the reason – the dog was missing a hind leg. Yet he stopped to be petted, wagged his tail and then trotted off, as if having three legs instead of four was nothing very exceptional.*
>
> *"The thought occurred to me that no one had told this brave little dog that he couldn't function minus a leg. He just went ahead and found a way to adjust to this loss and got on with his life. I also remembered the story of the man who felt sorry for himself because he had no shoes, until he met he met a man who had no feet. I realized this had been true for me in a very literal way. As I walked away from that meeting with the dog, I made a decision to stop seeing myself as a victim, and to start reaching out to others with greater suffering than my own. It was a life-changing moment for me."*

This man now does volunteer work in a hospital and has brought much comfort and healing to people in pain. His own hurts are also gradually being healed.

This man's experience can be a valuable lesson for us. Going out of ourselves and helping others can be one of the most effective ways for us to release our negative focus and shift to a wider frame of reference which makes life bearable.

A woman in a workshop put it very succinctly,

> *"**Pain can make you bitter or better.** I know because I was very bitter as a young widow with no money and no job. But my grandmother supported me in every way possible, and she had been through many more ordeals than I had. She taught me to pray again and to believe that I had inherited her courage to make a new life for myself. She wiped away my tears and said that it was time to stop looking back and time to get to work. I did just that, and I thank God for the pain that brought that woman's wisdom into my life."*

I also remember a former Marine whose reaction to his wounding has been an inspiration. He told of the dramatic moment when he chose to live rather than die, and to release his bitterness. The war in Vietnam left him a partial cripple, able at times to function with crutches, but at others only from a wheelchair. He had suffered serious neurological damage which affected his back and legs. The pain at times was intense and often the medication seemed to offer little relief. But his mental anguish was even more painful. He felt as if his life was over at twenty-three.

Then one day he made his first choice. He crawled to the window ledge of his hospital room, prepared to push off and end his life. He permitted himself one brief prayer, "Oh God, if you exist give me a sign." At that moment his favorite nurse entered the room and, aware of his intentions, walked over to the window. She took him in her arms and gently pulled him back into the room. He said, "I saw her love and concern for me in her eyes, and I was a goner. I held her and cried for a long time. I can't explain how it happened, but I knew that if someone loved me enough to want to save me, I sure as hell was going to fight to save myself." He then made his second choice, to live.

Today he works in a Navy rehabilitation center, where he dispenses tough love to paraplegics. He pushes them and scolds and challenges them. He pulls them out of their self-pity and depression. He teases them and makes them laugh. Later they come to recognize the love behind his actions. His life, which was almost ended too soon, is full and even joyful. He still has to live with physical pain, but he now knows how to live with it.

And that may be the most important lesson of all. The stories I have recounted indicate that the individuals concerned were led from a negative obsession with their own pain into a life of dedication to others. The bridge to that new life was learning the secret of living with being wounded and the suffering that ensued. Each of these people found that just as we learn that we can skate by finding out how to skate, so too we learn that we can live with our wounding by learning how to live with our pain and suffering.

We abandon the myth that once we overcome a particular wounding that all will be smooth sailing. Instead we take courage from the fact that we know from experience that we can survive the wounding. We learn to seek compassionate companions for this difficult journey. They help us to shift our focus from the pain to our inner resources and our ability to move step-by-step out of the anguish into a new life.

Many years ago Clare Boothe Luce was asked about her conversion to Catholicism after the death of her young daughter in an automobile accident. The interviewer said, *"Mrs. Luce, I would imagine that your new-found faith has brought you much comfort since your daughter's untimely death."* Mrs. Luce responded, *"On the contrary, it has given me no comfort at all. What it has given me is strength. I know how to face the pain and live with it. I find that an even greater gift."*

Like Mrs. Luce, we may also discover the true value of wounding. It is the ability to learn how to face the pain and live with it.

CHAPTER FIVE

Some Small Steps

As a child it was great fun to imagine the features of the man in the moon and to play with thoughts of life on this mysterious globe in the night sky. The idea that a man would one day walk on the moon was beyond my childish fantasies.

Then came that event which I shall never forget. I was in the Chicago airport waiting for a plane when I met an old friend who reminded me that the moon landing was about to take place. We headed for one of the Executive Lounges where, despite the fact that we were neither executives nor members of the airline club, we were permitted to watch the moon landing on television. The scene is etched in my mind: the small table where we sat, the smoke-filled room, the buzz of excitement in the air, and the quickening of my heartbeat as Neil Armstrong descended the stairway of the spaceship touching the surface of the moon. And then his immortal words: "one small step for man; one giant leap for mankind."

As we all shared our excitement over this wondrous event, we were also admiring the bravery of the astronauts. The risks they took were great indeed, and they had to overcome not only their own fears but also the negative judgment of others as they faced the challenges of unknown outer space.

Today, many years later, my respect for those early space explorers is as deep as when I witnessed the moon landing. And at the same time the intervening years have given me examples of men and women today who have gained a similar kind of admiration and respect in my heart. These are not extraordinary people engaged in monumental missions. Rather, they are ordinary men and women facing extraordinary challenges with unusual courage, and taking risks that are for them "giant leaps."

I am reminded of a couple whose single life-goal is to find a bone marrow donor for their three year old daughter. Their beautiful home, car, and savings have been sacrificed to pay the hospital bills. Their assets now are their love, and an abiding hope that her life will be saved. Their courage has not been a gift provided to them. It has been earned. Like the astronauts they have had to face not only their own fears, but the negative attitudes and abundant advice of relatives and friends. They have learned that their great leap of faith has to be sustained by the small steps they must take each day.

I think also of two men who, during difficult economic times, chose to start their own small businesses. Sacrificing a regular paycheck for the dubious reward of creating a successful enterprise seemed to be a worthwhile risk, though one fraught with fear. Not only did they have to pay this high price, their wives and children also were affected. Both men also had to face naysayers who tried to discourage them from this choice. Their decision took great courage and self-confidence, as well as the outside support of loved ones.

One of the men said to me,

"Never in my life have I received so much advice from so many people. Most of it was an effort to urge me to drop the project. It made me really angry, especially since I hadn't asked for the advice in the first place."

His anger enabled him to tell these advisors that he needed to make his own decision and live with the results. He also learned to stop the flow of advice before it started. As people began to offer their advice he interrupted them by saying,

"I know you mean well, but I really don't want to hear your advice. Help me to make my own decision by keeping that advice to yourself."

And though he feared he might lose some friends by doing this, only one person took offense at his remarks. In other words, he learned that this small step took one part of the burden of fear from him. He realized that he had been accepting the negative advice and fears of other people and adding these to his own fears. He also found that he did not need to carry this extra burden as he was attempting to take the "giant leap." He added that his wife was his greatest support as he struggled with his choice.

Not all spouses are able to be equally supportive. Sometimes there is quite a difference in levels of comfort when facing the risks of a career change.

I think of a couple who faced this challenge recently. Prior to this crisis their marriage had been a relatively smooth one. They were able to make compromises over most issues and allow for differences in taste and preferences. Later they discovered that their accommodations had always been over things of minor value. A career change revealed serious differences in their abilities to tolerate the ambiguity of such a choice and their markedly differing perceptions of its impact on their lives. Tom, the husband, saw the advantages of new challenges and career advancement, while Joan, the wife, saw the problems of uprooting for herself and the children, and the insecurity of the change.

Their differences revealed a perfect example of opposites being attracted to each other. Tom's adventurous spirit brought new excitement to Joan's life, yet the crisis of a career change highlighted their differing abilities to handle unknown fears. Unless both persons can face their individual fears and learn to live and act with their fears, any choice made regarding the career runs the added risk of seriously impairing the relationship. It is possible with counseling to overcome this obstacle, but its importance should not be overlooked.

Having to choose, to decide upon one thing, reveals our level of comfort even in small matters. A client once said to me, "I could go through life contented, as long as I had someone else to make decisions for me." And a friend confessed, "I dread having to choose between two things. Give me five or six choices and it's easy. Give me two, and my mind is filled with confusion. I just cannot decide." Yet another person will have the opposite reaction. Give him two choices and he has no problem. Give him ten and he has great difficulty making a selection. It is called the Candy Store Syndrome.

Small challenges in decision-making do not affect our lives to any great degree, but our difficulty in making such choices can furnish us with information about our pattern of choosing and illuminate our level of tolerance for risk in more important life choices. It can also reveal the nature of our underlying fears.

For one person, it may be the fear of failure. For another, the fear of accepting responsibility, or the fear of appearing foolish. Many fears have their roots in childhood experiences, and represent the voices of authority figures casting doubt on our ability or self-worth. These set our level of risk taking at a low notch, and help to explain our paralysis in decision-making. Only by facing these fears can we free ourselves.

Confronting our fears is one of the small steps towards enabling us to make whatever "great leap" may be required. Gloria Steinem said that she found the courage to choose by asking herself what would be the worst thing that could happen to her if she took the planned risk. Her answer was that she could end up as a bag lady on the street. And as she imagined that actually happening, she discovered that she would probably find a way to organize the other bag ladies. Confronting the "worst" helps to change a catastrophic expectation to an unpleasant experience that is manageable.

Fritz Perls, the father of Gestalt Therapy, offered a suggestion to make this confrontation easier. He proposed that we become aware of feelings of excitement that accompany the fear. By focusing our attention on these feelings, we release energy which permits us to examine our fears without being dominated by them. This may seem to be a rather strange suggestion, but it actually can have a powerful effect on us, lessening the impact and paralysis of fear in decision-making.

Another small step is to face our fears with support. This kind of safety net is used successfully by AA, drug rehabilitation groups, and encounter groups. A spouse, close friend or therapist can offer support which allows us to share our fear and renew our sense of self-confidence. As we have seen, support has nothing to do with a value judgment about the choice. Support says, "I love you and respect your right to make your own choice, and I will assist you in any way you deem helpful."

Learning to ask for support rather than advice is also important. A friend of mine does this very simply. He says, "Will you help me look at this decision? I need to talk out my fears and concerns so I can understand what is involved. I don't want any advice, just your listening and support." It usually works well for him. This kind of loving, non-judging companionship, frees us to contact our own inner sources of wisdom rather than the opinions of outside authority figures, whether past or present. It is perhaps the most valuable small step that we can take in making an important life choice.

Facing our fears with support permits us to ask different questions of ourselves. Our fears suggest the question, "What if I take this risk?" with the implication that something disastrous could happen. The support suggests a different question, "What if I don't take this risk?," implying opportunities missed, and rewards not obtained.

Surveys of famous people revealed that their only regrets about previous decisions, were about risks they had not taken. Some said they regretted allowing a choice to be made by default, simply allowing time to run out. They came to realize the truth of Harvey Cox's famous line, "Not to choose is to choose." The author of *The Secular City* knew from experience that the choice not to risk may in the end be the riskiest choice of all. Delaying, holding back when it is time to move on, may be the source of deep regret later. Indeed, as the poet has said, the saddest words of all are "what might have been."

Anne Morrow Lindbergh, in her book *Gift From The Sea,* reminds us that nature can be a wonderful source of insight enabling us to overcome our basic fear of change. She tells of a lesson learned from examining seashells: shells are temporary shelters not lifetime dwelling places. They are not intended to provide permanent security for their inhabitants. Sometimes the shell no longer fits. It becomes too cramped an environment for further growth, and so the crab or sea snail, accepting it as a fact of life rather than a tragedy, simply moves on to another, more accommodating shelter. The author suggests that this may be a metaphor for human existence as well.

Sometimes as we grow and change, we outgrow friendships, careers and intimate relationships. Viewing our human connections as gifts for the present, rather than solid assurances for the future, can make the decision to risk change easier for us. This attitude can be another small step towards a new and rewarding life experience.

Once we confront our fear of change and of the unknown we can move out of the paralysis of indecision. Fear breeds in confusion and mental imaginings of negative possibilities. These in turn can furnish us with countless excuses for remaining undecided. Often this mental paralysis can be overcome only by taking some action. "Just do it!" is often a wise response.

David K. Reynolds, influenced by many years of study in Japan, suggests the path of "Constructive Living" as opposed to feeling victimized and helpless in the face of a difficult choice. This is a path of action, of "doing what needs to be done" even while fearful. It means acknowledging the fear and moving ahead at the same time.

The action need not be a great leap. It can be a small step, but doing something rather than thinking about doing something is a movement forward. Growth is accomplished in small increments. Change is achieved by small steps taken with care and supported by whatever means are required: one step at a time, one step after another.

This path is one which can lead us out of our dark frightening forest into a clearing where we can see the path leading toward our promising future. The great leaps will take care of themselves if we can hold in our hearts the inspiring truth expressed in the Tao Te Ching: **"The journey of a thousand miles begins with one step."**

CHAPTER SIX

The Other Side

At a Town Hall Meeting several years ago the moderator held up an object about the size of a tennis ball. He asked the audience to tell him the color of the ball. With one voice they shouted, "White!" He then asked the panel of speakers seated on the stage behind him, and they replied, "Black!" By turning the ball around several times, both groups could see that the ball was half white and half black.

The purpose of this demonstration was to remind us that in discussions we can easily fall into the trap of thinking that our perception is the only true reality. In actuality, we may only be seeing a limited view of an issue, and the full truth may only be found when we can view it from all sides. There is invariably an "other side" to objects as well as to issues and concerns.

Conflict so often arises when people view a situation from differing perspectives, certain that their individual perceptions and the ensuing judgments are correct.

A well-known documentary film entitled, *The Eye of the Beholder,* dramatizes this phenomenon. A number of people witness a violent interaction and are later asked to describe what they saw. As they report their impressions, it becomes apparent that they are describing their reactions to the scene rather than reporting factual observations.

This characteristic of people presents problems for lawyers and jurors in courtroom testimony. When our emotional reactions are especially strong, we are inclined to color our judgments by passing our observations through specific emotional filters. Often we do this without being aware of the process of colorization. In trying to determine the full truth, it is most helpful to remind ourselves that despite the strength of our feeling reactions, most likely there are several other sides that need to be examined.

Reality and truth are seldom simple, unequivocal concepts when applied to human experience. They are rarely black or white, all good or all bad, absolutely right or completely wrong.

In the martial art of Aikido, the successful person is one who is able to resist the temptation to take a rigid position even in the face of an attack. He learns to maintain balance while artfully allowing the blows to be deflected. He is able to sense the movement of his opponent, to "take in" the various sides of this physical issue. His secret is in maintaining his balance while dealing with these many differing approaches.

This is a valuable lesson for everyone. **Balance is the key to truth rather than one rigid position or judgment.** Balance can be experienced only after examining many different sides of an issue, and measuring their worth and integrity. We begin that process by recognizing from the outset that there are other sides and perceptions and that we want to learn from these, as well as from our own knowledge and experience.

One approach to this learning is to look at the emphasis in counseling on the positive aspects of growth. We recognize the value of a good self-image, as well as the ability to be a self-starter. We have learned that it can be good to ask for what we want, to take risks, to trust our inner wisdom, and to be responsible for our own actions. Indeed these are important concepts. And it is also true that they represent only one side of the coin of growth.

The other side, one often overlooked or neglected, reveals aspects that are equally important and which offer a valuable counter-balance to the merely positive, proactive side. For instance, a positive self-image is built principally from messages of self received from others. Learning to accept help can be as valuable as struggling to act alone. Being sensitive to the needs of others and reaching out to those in need can be as necessary for our maturity as having the courage to ask for our own needs.

Holding back, being patient, and postponing pleasure, can be as rewarding as learning to take risks. Listening to the wisdom and experience of others can often contain the key to the treasure house of our own inner source of wisdom.

Being self-sufficient is wonderful, and equally wonderful is being able to surrender. Surrender is not a negative concept when it is a responsible choice. I recall a Hawaiian surfer who demonstrated this when he was swept out to sea by a powerful riptide. He said,

> *"I started to panic, to fight the current, and then I remembered that to fight could be fatal. So I surrendered to the current and let myself by carried by its flow. I was taken almost a mile down the coast. Then the currents changed and I could swim back to shore. It*

was a powerful lesson for me: to know when to struggle and when to surrender."

Holding on to attitudes and values is also important, yet the other side of this virtue is the ability to let go. As we grow it is necessary to re-examine our values and long-held notions. They may no longer have the same meaning for us or prove to be helpful. Some men and women will cling to ideas and judgments they acquired as children and cannot let go of them. This happens frequently in families where there have been serious misunderstandings and angry conflicts.

Parents or children may hang on to their resentment and bitterness, refusing to go beyond their feelings of being victims in the family tragedy. Each side feels justified in keeping the hurt and anger alive, not realizing that they are increasing the pain by their unwillingness to let go of the injured feelings.

One woman said, "I just cannot forgive my daughter for the hurt and shame she has brought upon the family." And her daughter said something very similar, "I don't think I will ever forgive my mother for not coming to help me when I needed her." Both have adopted rigid positions of right and wrong, and inflict more pain on themselves by their rigidity. When they can begin to recognize what they are doing, it is then possible for them to alter their fixed attitudes and move toward more compassionate responses.

A physician friend of mine is especially gifted in helping people to let go of their fear and long-held resentments. Retired from active medical practice, he continued to see patients in his home, and primarily functioned as a caring therapist. One afternoon, at sunset, I sat with him on his pool deck, from which we could see the ocean and the clouds colored by the setting sun. It was beautiful and peaceful and we spent a few moments in silent enjoyment of the scene.

I asked him to tell me how he worked with these patients and he said,

> *"I see only a couple of people each day, and these are referred to me. I give them as much time as they need, and I do not charge them. I feel this is my gift in gratitude for the blessings I have received.*
>
> *"All that I do is invite them to tell me their life story, and I listen to them. In essence, I offer them my attention and my love, and they respond to this very positively. Gradually they begin to let go of their fear and are able to restore feelings of hope and strength. I am certain that these men and women have never experienced the satisfaction of having someone really listen to their inner hurt. And being listened to, without judgment, enabled them to release their rigid hold on old pain and bitterness.*
>
> *"I sincerely believe the phrase from the Bible that says, 'perfect love casts out fear,' because I have seen it happen over and over."*

His words echo the sentiments of Gerald Jampolsky who entitled his book, *Love is Letting Go of Fear.* Once the rigid attitude is released, other feelings, ideas and possibilities become available to us. It is as if our mind has been enclosed in a tunnel, with only one view in sight, and that one rather dark. The experience of being heard, understood, accepted and loved is like opening the door of our prison and bringing us into the sun-filled world of beauty and hope.

I recently spoke with a man who had spent ten years in prison. He said that when he entered prison as a young man in his early twenties he had a very narrow vision of what his life could be. He was concerned about stealing enough money to support his drug habit, and that was his only focus and concern.

Several years later, after drug rehab, he worked with a counselor who had led a similar existence at one time. The counselor offered the young man tough love. He did not accept excuses and sometimes scolded, but he was also generous with his praise and understanding. The young man discovered a new sense of self, freedom to choose the way he would act, and a desire to emulate his counselor in creating a rewarding life for himself.

He is now a computer expert who spends many hours coaching basketball for underprivileged children. Other options became available as he let go of his old fears and feelings of insecurity. He had to ask for help to overcome his addiction, and understand himself, but having asked he was able to receive the love that liberated him, even before he was freed from the prison.

I remember well an incident from counseling that freed me from one of my own rigidities. From childhood I had learned to be punctual. I was quite proud of my record of being on time for appointments. On this occasion I was to meet a man at seven o'clock in the evening for a counseling session. The hour came and he did not appear. Just after seven-thirty, I was preparing to leave the office when he arrived. He rushed past me into the office and sat down without a word of greeting. I sensed his tension, but I was somewhat irritated by his lack of greeting.

The irritation prompted my first remark, "You're late!" His response was immediate, "Yes, and you're the second person that has scolded me today for being late." I was not proud of my scolding, but I felt ashamed by my immediate insensitivity as I sensed that this man was deeply troubled. Hearing the hurt and frustration in his voice, I spoke in a more kindly way. "I'm sorry about that remark. It sounds as if you have had a terrible day, but would you mind telling me about it?"

He described an incident earlier in the day when he drove a colleague to the repair shop to pick up his car. The trip took longer than expected and he was late for a faculty meeting at his school, and thus the first scolding by the principal. Along with other minor crises, it was not one of his better days.

After listening to this tale of frustration I said to him, "So then, after all that, you come to see me, expecting me to be someone who is understanding and caring, and the first thing I do is to give you another scolding. If I had been in your place I would have felt really depressed." He smiled and said, "I was, but I'm not now, and I appreciate your apology. I would like to get past that and work on some issues that are very important to me."

Then he shared some very painful moments from his adolescence, adding that it was the first time he had dared to face these scars in his memory. We did some role playing and fantasy work, and he was able to begin the healing of those old wounds. We continued the process for several weeks, by which time he felt secure enough to end counseling.

Several years later we met at a conference in Mexico and agreed to have breakfast together. The next morning he smiled broadly as he gave me a hug and said, "You will notice that I am on time." I said, "I noticed." During breakfast he told me what a powerful impact that counseling session had on him, as well as being touched by the fact that I would apologize to him.

I told him I was happy to hear of his growth and his own work as a counselor. And then I said to him, "You know the impact on you, but I would like to tell you of the impact of that session on me. Ever since then I have been free of my rigid demand that others maintain the same punctuality that I hold myself to. I realize that there are dozens of reasons why people are late, some of their choosing and some not. I can let them arrive at their own time and be at peace with their schedule. You gave me the gift of viewing the other side of the issue of time, and I shall always be grateful for that gift." It has indeed been a blessing for me through the years.

As a child I was fortunate to spend time with my parents in the California desert, and I learned much about the unique aspects of nature in a desert environment. The desert can be a formidable place, dangerous in many ways. Poisonous snakes and scorpions abound. The weather can change from scorching days to freezing nights. It can appear to be an enemy of man. Then a sudden rainstorm can sweep across the desert floor flooding the surface sand and creating new riverbeds as the sand absorbs the rain. And when the skies have cleared, the miracle appears.

As far as the eye can see, the desert is filled with color: There are green shrubs and desert flowers in a variety of shades carpeting the desert sands. The sweet fragrance of sagebrush fills the air and makes one want to breathe deeply of its freshness. This is one of the "other" sides of the desert, a gift of beauty for the beholder, even amidst the dangerous aspects of the environment.

I believe this metaphor applies to life situations that seem formidable, things we label as tragedies, failures or apparently hopeless problems. **The caring words and kind, often generous, actions of others can be like gentle rain** which falls gracefully upon the desert of our lives, ready to nurture our souls.

This gift, if we allow it to enter into our hearts can bring us renewed patience as we learn that we can survive and find peace even in the midst of a desert.

Hope springs anew, and once again we experience the beauty that surrounds us and lives within us.

CHAPTER SEVEN

Try A Bit of Craziness

The language of love is unique. Lyrics of songs speak of being "madly in love," "crazy for you," "out of my mind" and other expressions that suggest a kind of passion that is a form of insanity. Lovers describe themselves as captivated, obsessed and crazed by love. But anyone who has been deeply in love understands this dramatic language. It is the passion of love that makes us feel and act a bit crazed.

Recently I listened to a man describe his current madness. It was a familiar story. He was in love with a woman who did not return his love. The more she resisted his advances, the more determined he became to win her heart. Gifts, flowers, love letters, phone calls failed to achieve the goal. He could neither eat nor sleep, and was obsessed with his desire for this woman. At the moment this man was incapable of accepting the fact of her lack of attraction to him, nor could he view this experience as a wonderful gift for the future.

As an outside observer who knows a bit about this man's life, I can see some valuable lessons that can be growth points for him. As a child he was seen as a "good boy," obedient and reserved. Even in his teenage years he engaged in very little rebellion, emerging into adulthood with well-controlled emotions, few friends, and little excitement in his life. Falling in love with a beautiful woman allowed him to throw caution aside, and pursue this woman with a kind of wild abandon. For the first time passion entered his life, not merely sexual passion, but a passion for living, a sense of 'joie de vivre.' It was a disturbing, yet exciting experience.

Hopefully, with a little time and some healing, he will be able to view his madness as a powerful mentor for him, a loving teacher who revealed new depths of his personality and rich emotions which were now able to be expressed. The lesson for him as well as for all of us is that a little craziness can also be a valuable gift for us.

We may even be able to view the concept of craziness differently. Our culture has maintained a great fear of mental illness. We have developed a paranoia about people who are paranoid. Today, experts are recognizing that mental illness may in actuality be a survival mechanism. It is a way for people to survive in what seems to them to be a crazy world.

The human organism has endlessly creative ways to protect itself from perceived harm. The body marshals its immunological system to war against infection and disease, and in a similar way the human spirit summons the will to live and finds ways to cope with emotional overload. Amnesia, denial, loss of feeling, and schizophrenia can be responses to pain and trauma that appear too great to handle. From this perspective, crazy behavior can be seen not as sick or inappropriate, but rather as a necessary and even creative survival mechanism.

In fact, anyone who has worked in a mental institution can verify the fact that the patients are remarkably creative in getting attention, in dramatizing their needs and hoodwinking their caretakers. For many, these talents were not tapped before entering the institution. It seems that their will to survive activated an inner core of intelligence and imagination. A therapist may be able to redirect this creative ability towards activities that will move the person towards the path of health.

I recall a client who demonstrated this. In our first session he said that he had been hospitalized recently for severe stress, but felt that he needed some help to rebuild his life. His chief concerns were his troubled marriage and occasional periods of depression. At some point in the session his words became jumbled and I could not make sense of them. Listening closely I realized that he had moved into some secret compartment of his mind apart from me. After a few minutes he would take up his former conversation as if nothing unusual had occurred. The experience was a new one for me, and I felt unqualified to deal with it. I resolved to refer him to a capable psychiatrist.

Toward the end of the session the client mentioned that he also wanted to lose some weight. Together we examined some possible changes in diet and exercise. I decided to wait until the end of the second session to refer him. To my surprise he arrived for his second session saying that he felt much better. He had lost two pounds, slept peacefully, and felt hopeful for the first time in many months.

His attention often wandered during our sessions. Sometimes he would not talk and sat in silence. I did not say anything judgmental. We talked briefly about whatever he wanted to discuss, and mostly sat in silence together. I felt that our supportive therapy was helping rather than harming him.

Gradually he began to speak more and retreated into silence less. After three months of working together he felt secure enough to leave counseling. At our last session he said something that made a lasting impression on me. He said, "I know you felt uneasy when I 'went away' during our sessions because you didn't know where I was. I didn't know where I was either, and what made me feel secure was that sense that wherever I was, you were there with me. I could be a little crazy and know you were right there if I needed you."

Apparently it was important for him to permit himself to act crazed and not be judged by someone. Gradually the need to protect himself in this way lessened as he felt safe in the supportive counseling environment. He found that he could use his creativity in healthier ways. Within several months he had begun a new career, repaired his marriage, and felt confident as he faced the future.

I was able to be in contact with him for a number of years and looked forward to his amusing letters at Christmas, illustrated by his clever sketches. From the vantage point of time it is clear that his craziness was not only a necessity at one period in his life, it was also a great gift to him. By responding to an inner impulse for survival, he was later able to uncover a creative potential that allowed him to take control of his life with confidence for the future.

Craziness can serve a useful purpose in our lives. It can bring us to the awareness of inner resources. Perhaps we are too quick to label a new adventure or a risky decision as crazy.

Often during counseling sessions, I have asked men and women to describe their secret desires. I say, "If you could wave the magic wand and create whatever you wish, what would that be?" Most often they will respond shyly with an introductory apology, "Well, this may sound crazy but..."

Their wish does not sound crazy at all, but they feel a little guilty for wanting something that seems so foreign to their ordinary humdrum lives. Often they experience lives of quiet desperation, yet secretly yearn for excitement and adventure. It is only their fears that tell them they cannot hope for more than they presently have.

Whose are these voices that make us feel so helpless and impoverished? Are they the voices of parents, teachers, friends, or of the culture in which we were reared? We spend so many years being rewarded for conformity that it can be difficult to find and hear our own inner voice, which contains wisdom peculiar to our lives, our hopes and dreams.

It may be time to question our response to life, and our fears that prompt us to follow the norms and judgments of others. I have discovered that advice given by friends and loved ones tells us more about their fears than it does about the appropriateness of our actions. "I think you would be foolish to choose that course," when translated really says, "I would be afraid to choose that course because I would fear looking foolish." It may be time to risk a little craziness, to dare to be a little different, to try something new.

At a number of periods in life we come to important choice-points that offer us new challenges. Perhaps we have accomplished all that is possible in a career or a relationship, and it is time to move on. A friend said to me recently,

"I suddenly became aware that I was forty-five years of age and had never owned a sporty car. When I was younger I couldn't afford it, and later I was afraid people would say I was having a mid-life crisis. But then I realized that it was the fulfillment of a childhood fantasy for a child who had been deprived of many things.

"I went out and bought an expensive red convertible and loved the thrill of driving that car and enjoying the envious glances of people who saw me. And I did not mind the head-shaking of people who thought I was crazy. The real learning for me was that it was not the car I had desired, it was the freedom to choose that kind of a car despite the fear of what other people would think.

"As a matter of fact, after a few months I found that the convertible was too windy and the roof leaked when it rained, so I sold it. But I'm still glad I felt free to buy it."

The courage to be a little crazy, to change our lives in a significant way, can begin with small steps in that direction. A friend of mine who was unhappy in his career took a course in massage, which was judged as a crazy choice by his friends. From this initial step he enrolled in other workshops, learning to confront his fears as well as discovering some hidden talents. He found that he had a unique ability to work with people in conflict situations. With training he became a management consultant specializing in conflict resolution.

Today he smiles at his early "craziness" saying,

"Even I feared I was acting crazed, but now I am so grateful for the courage to take those initial risks. It was as if my heart knew what I needed and wanted, and when I could follow it, I realized my hidden dreams of success."

Craziness, even when referring to neurosis or psychosis, can at times be not only a survival tool, but also a gift for later life. And craziness, when applied to actions that appear foolish or inappropriate to others, can similarly be a response to the cry of our inner spirit for liberation and rebirth. **It may be time to listen to our own inner voice urging us to "try a bit of craziness."**

CHAPTER EIGHT

Following Your Heart

Once during an encounter group session, I saw the facilitator go over to the side of a man who had been describing great personal anguish. He took the man in his arms and held him and soon the man was sobbing. This gesture enabled the man to release emotions that had been pent-up for years, and was the prelude to new growth for him.

When I later asked the facilitator what had prompted him to offer the gesture he replied, "I was very touched by his inner pain, and I simply followed my heart." My reaction to his statement was admiration for his courage. I too had been touched by the man's pain, but I could not have imagined myself hugging the man. I would have felt it intrusive, and being rather shy I would have refrained from such a personal response. Looking back I now see that in truth I envied the facilitator; he had listened to his heart and I had listened to my fear.

Since that time I have been less timid in my responses to people in need. I have learned to listen more with my heart than with my head, and to follow my heart in making a response. The lesson for me has been a surprising one. I have discovered that my heart triggers my intuition and makes it possible to hear the need of a person which often cannot be expressed in words. And a further lesson learned is the realization that, more often than not, the response is appropriate and welcomed. I have also formed enduring friendships by overcoming my fear and following my heart.

An example is a friendship that began from an article in a paper. I read of the organization that two women had founded to care for children displaced by World War II. They were able to place hundreds of boys and girls in convents and monasteries throughout Europe, and to raise funds to care for them. I was touched by their generosity and courage and called to express my admiration for their work. Invited to visit them, I learned more about their remarkable experiences during and after the war. In turn, I offered to help them with some of their correspondence and business affairs, and ran their office while they were in Europe.

The friendship deepened as I accompanied them on several trips and experienced first-hand the impact of their caring upon the lives of so many unfortunate children. I also discovered the fact that both of these women had followed the direction of their hearts, as they responded to a plea from some Catholic nuns in Europe asking for help in caring for these orphaned children.

The difficulties and red tape they had to overcome were immense, but their reward was the satisfaction of seeing the children safe and cared for. They also became role models for others in the huge task of saving children from the ravages of post-war Europe.

I now smile as I recall my initial fear of contacting them, thinking they were important, busy women who would not want to be bothered by an admiring fan. The reality was that they appreciated my interest and from them I learned more about the value of following one's heart.

I received another lesson in the value of listening to one's heart, when as a young man I attended a concert of Artur Rubinstein in the Hollywood Bowl. I was the guest of a family friend who invited me backstage to meet the celebrated pianist. And while I was excited at the prospect, I was fearful that I would not know what to say, and suggested it might be better for her to go alone. She looked directly at me and said, "You are shy about meeting this great man, aren't you?" I nodded in agreement, and then she said, "What does your heart tell you?" I replied, "It tells me I want to meet him." And with that she led me backstage.

It happened they were old friends, and this woman introduced me in Spanish. I responded in my impoverished Spanish, apologizing for my inadequate vocabulary. Rubinstein laughed and said, "Ah, but my friend, we all stumble a bit when we learn a new language. You have a good accent. Do study it and practice, just as I have to continue to study and practice on the piano." And then as he signed my program he said to me, "Your last name is so short. I must sign Rubinstein over and over. I wish mine were as short as yours."

The exchange was very brief, but the impact has lasted all my life. I treasure his graciousness to an embarrassed young man. The memory of that first meeting came to mind again when shortly before his death I was able, through the gift of a friend, to attend the seventieth anniversary of his debut in Carnegie Hall. He played an inspired program, and I echoed the sentiment of a critic who wrote: "Last night, Carnegie Hall was awash in love." This great pianist was also a wonderful, humble, gracious human being who could make a shy young man feel at ease. And I have often thanked my friend for encouraging me to listen to my heart and helping me to overcome an unreasonable shyness.

These examples indicate how even small fears can lead to rich life experiences if we listen to our hearts rather than our heads. This is especially true when we face important life choices. Our heads can suggest countless reasons for not choosing a certain way. They can marshal logical pros and cons which seem very appealing. However, what our heads offer us is a decision based on what we ought to do, rather than what we truly want to do. That choice must come, ultimately, from the heart rather than the head.

This may help to explain why so many men and women are miserable in their careers, feeling more like persons trapped in their jobs, than nurtured and satisfied by them. The heart must be consulted if we are to be genuinely happy in our careers. There is a slogan which expresses this reality in blunt terms: "If you don't love your work, get out of it, or it will kill you."

This heart-listening does not always result in a complete career change. At times it can simply be the addition of something that will make our lives more rewarding. Recently a man in Hawaii was interviewed about his work with AIDS patients. He made good money as a construction worker but felt a lack of satisfaction from his job. When his younger brother became ill with AIDS he helped take care of the brother for two years prior to his death. Afterwards he volunteered to help other AIDS patients and he spoke of the impact on him.

"I had never been around people who were so sick, and had never seen someone die. The only way I can explain my wanting to help in this way is that my heart was touched. I knew I could be a companion to them, and let them know I cared. And their real gratitude touched me even more. I believe I got far more from them than I gave."

This appears to be a special blessing resulting from listening to one's heart—the impulse to respond to others in need with greater generosity and selflessness. And frequently this is the best therapy for our own problems and inner pain.

Volunteers who have worked in the clinic of Mother Teresa have given eloquent witness to this phenomenon. Many arrived at the clinic with heavy personal burdens, but in the process of caring for the poor and sick, especially the children, their values shifted and their own personal problems seemed lighter and less desperate. The work, which at first seemed so challenging, became for many an experience in self-sacrifice that brought an inner joy previously unknown to them.

Norman Cousins illustrates this point with a story of a visit he made to a Veterans Hospital. He had been invited to give a talk to a group of cancer patients in the hope that he could improve their low morale. The setting was rather formal: an auditorium, a panel of doctors seated on a stage, a lectern and microphone for him, and the audience seated in chairs below.

Cousins gave an entertaining talk, stressing the importance of laughter in the healing process, and at the end suggested a project for the group. He asked them to collect together their various talents and to put on a show for the entertainment of the other hospital patients. Several weeks later Cousins returned to learn of the results.

This time, there was no panel or microphone. Instead, the doctors had joined the patients in small groups, and Cousins was invited to sit in with one of the groups. The facilitator explained that they met this way regularly and they began the session by sharing some amusing or happy experience from the past week. Cousins himself had a couple of amusing incidents to relate when it was his turn.

In telling the story later, he said that the change in morale and attitude was dramatic. In putting on the show, the men had learned of hidden talents of one another, had discovered the satisfaction of creating something together, and were touched by the delight and applause of the patients they entertained. By going out of themselves to offer a gift to others in pain, they found their own gift of inner joy.

Sometimes following your heart can seem a dangerous choice, yet I am continually surprised at the rewards people report from taking the risk. A woman told me of her experience at work. Her boss was a very demanding woman and on one occasion had scolded this woman harshly for some error. The woman felt humiliated and angry until a sudden insight struck her. She said to herself, "Thelma is a very lonely, unhappy woman."

This thought changed her anger to feelings of compassion, and she resolved to follow her heart in responding to her boss. A week later, as Thanksgiving was approaching, she found a clever card with a witty cartoon and placed the card on Thelma's desk during the lunch break. When her boss returned she could hear peals of laughter coming from her office. The next day she found a card on her desk thanking her and wishing her a happy holiday.

It was the beginning of an ongoing exchange of amusing cards, which became a kind of gentle, caring dialogue between the two women. They never socialized outside the office, but when the woman retired her boss made it a point to publicly thank her saying, "You have made my life so much more enjoyable by your friendship." This is a remarkable example of a small gesture bearing abundant rewards.

Upon reflection, we may discover that our reluctance to follow our heart reflects a kind of arrogance which assumes that we always know what is the best course of action. Genuine humility recognizes that the universe may have some surprises for us which promote our growth in ways we would never devise.

Several years ago I met a priest in Rome who related his own life lesson in this regard. During World War II, Monsignor Patrick Carroll-Abbing was assigned to an office in the Vatican. A rather shy Irishman by nature, he found it painful to walk the streets of Rome and see the poverty and hunger of the local people.

One day he came across a group of small boys huddled together in an alley, sharing a tiny crust of bread. He realized that these were part of the famous "Shoeshine Boys," vagabonds, many of them orphans, and most of them already criminals. He described the meeting,

> *"They seemed so young, like little children, most were under eight years of age. Their faces were grimy and their clothes mere tatters, and they looked at me*

with fear in their eyes. They had learned to trust no one.

"I told them I would try to find some bread for them and return at the same hour the following day. I don't think they believed me, but the next day they sent two boys to meet me and accepting the bag of bread, darted off in the alley. I brought them food begged from our kitchen, and those of friends, for several weeks. The group of boys grew in size and although I told myself I should not get involved with these boys, I felt sorry for them, as they seemed so vulnerable.

"Then I asked a kindly woman who lived in the area if she would be willing to make a pot of soup daily, if I brought the vegetables. Gradually friends helped, and the boys had at least one decent meal a day. Later I found an abandoned house outside Rome, and with help from friends and the labors of the boys we turned it into a shelter where they could stay at night, with an adult to oversee them. It was the beginning of what is now known as the Italian Boys Town, with over two hundred boys in residence. They have their own mayor, run several businesses, and solve their problems by themselves. I am simply their 'Papa,' who loves them and supports them."

As we were speaking, one of the young boys came up to the Monsignor and was received with a hug and a tousling of the hair, and when the boy had left us I asked him how he was able to overcome his initial shyness to be so openly affectionate with the boys. He said,

"At first it was very difficult, but I realized that these boys needed these expressions of love more than they needed bread. I was then able to freely offer food for

their hearts and souls." He paused, and then looking at me directly said, "Please do not misunderstand. You may think I have been some kind of hero, saving the lives of these boys, but the truth is that they have given meaning to mine, and enriched me beyond words with their love."

It might appear that following your heart is simply an excuse for doing whatever you want. But there is a world of difference between an impulse that comes from desire and one that arises from compassion. One is self-centered and the other is directed towards something outside us. Desire makes us want; compassion makes us want to do for others.

At first, as we experiment with following the heart, we may make an occasional mistake of judgment. We are not perfect. But it has been my experience that the heart contains the key to true wisdom and the path to inner peace. The rewards of following this path are like those of finding a buried treasure within. Our compassion deepens, our generosity increases, and our life has genuine meaning and purpose.

The biblical phrase is most apt, **"Where your heart is, there your treasure lies."**

CHAPTER NINE

If At First...

Recently a local Hawaiian radio station recognized a need and found a way to meet it. Aware of the importance of a high school prom as a part of the ritual of growing up, they surveyed their listeners to discover how many still felt cheated over their prom experience. Some did not go because they were not invited. Others did not have the money. Some said their parents refused to allow them to attend.

Then there were those who did go and had a terrible or sad experience. They complained that their dates got drunk or flirted with other persons; they felt mismatched, alienated, or just plain bored.

In both instances, for those who could not attend, but wanted to, and those who did attend and wished they had not, the high school prom was a great source of disappointment tinged with regret. The "highlight of my life" turned out to be the "low point of my adolescence." The prom experience was not one they wanted to repeat.

Then the radio station created a program called *Second Chance.* The aim was to invite selected listeners to a Prom Evening at an elegant hotel, with dinner and dancing provided. They would have an opportunity to create a prom of their own, a chance to have the pleasant kind of experience that they failed to have in their adolescence. The stories told on the radio program are amazing: couples re-united after many years; new lovers wanting to capture that special experience missed when they were younger; men and women eager to have this second chance, and planning creative ways to make it an especially enjoyable occasion. The program has been enormously successful.

It also underlines a very important issue. All too often, we deny ourselves a second, third or fourth chance because either we don't believe it is possible to have another chance, or we feel that we may not even deserve it. So often in counseling, men and women "give in" when they should "hang in," or give up when they should try again. Sometimes an inspiring example will give us that extra energy to hold on, and to make a new effort to be successful.

A few years ago, a Vietnamese-born young man was one of the graduates in the Maui, Hawaii police department class. Six years earlier he had come from Vietnam. He was sixteen years old. Through the help of a physician in Hawaii, he came to Hawaii and eventually was adopted by the physician and his family. He finished high school with great difficulty because of the language barrier, but his faith was strong that he would overcome the obstacles toward his goal of becoming a policeman. His driving force was the belief that he had been given a second chance at life. Had he stayed in Vietnam he was sure he would have been imprisoned and perhaps killed.

After failing the first test, he studied English with great intensity, and was able to be successful in the second test for the police department. He admits that the initial training was very hard, as is his ongoing adjustment to the cultural differences in America. But he is now grateful for the past, even the hard work to come to this country and the training to become a police officer. In an interview he said, "I love this country and am grateful to it for giving me freedom." As his eyes filled with tears he said, "It is my country now, my home, and I am going to work hard to be a good citizen, and a good policeman." Eloquent testimony to the importance of not giving up, and of seizing the opportunity for a second chance at life.

Having the opportunity presented is no less important than having the courage to act upon it. A number of years ago, a woman widowed by the war with a child to support and only a small savings account, realized she had to create a new life. Since she had no marketable skills, she decided to invest her savings in a large house and to rent out rooms. She bought and furnished a house and soon had the rooms rented to young working men. They were steady renters, in part because she also served them dinner, and she was an excellent cook.

A friend told her of a smaller house nearby that was for sale, and since she had some extra savings she decided to buy it, and have her young men help her to repair and decorate it. When it was finished she had a party for everyone to celebrate. Within a few months she sold the house for twice the amount she paid for it and a new career was born.

For fifty years she bought "fixer-upper" houses, repaired them with the help of her renters, and added her own decorative touches. She sold them for a modest profit and often said, "I learned not to be greedy. I was content to take a small profit, rather than wait for a killing. I turned the money into another purchase, fixed it up, and made another small profit."

Her daughter followed her example, and both ended up millionaires.

Later the daughter remarked about her mother's courage in re-directing her life. She said,

> *"My mother took a great risk in buying that first house for investment. She had no idea that it would lead to a wonderful and exciting career. She found a way to express her artistic talents as well as learning a great deal about the economics of buying and selling homes. It was a risky choice but a rewarding one for her. It was also, for both of us a chance to have new careers."*

Unfortunately, many of us fail to grab the brass ring as the merry-go-round of life offers it to us. Fear and indecision allow it to pass us by. However, there is always another turn of the merry-go-round, always a second chance and more to stir up our courage and take the risk of trying something new. The main obstacle we face is our refusal to believe that one failure does not mean the end of opportunity. Believing in the possibility of a second chance makes us receptive when it appears before us. And sometimes we need to prepare ourselves by taking some steps in the direction we hope will lead to this discovery.

A young office worker came to this awareness. He felt stifled by his present job and yet felt trapped in it. With a wife and small child, he did not have the courage to quit and look for another job. Then he asked himself what steps he might take that would make such a change possible. His answer was an economic solution. He estimated that if he could save five hundred dollars, he would have enough money to survive for a month. (This was over fifty years ago when that was a fair amount of money!)

With the support of his wife, they found many ways to save small amounts of money. He gave up cigarettes, took a sack lunch to work, and cut back on many small luxuries. His wife similarly saved on food and household expenses. They put the money in a savings account in the Chase National Bank of New York. Finally, after many months they had accumulated the five hundred dollars.

At that point he walked in to his office manager and announced that he was quitting. He later described what happened. " I told the boss that I was leaving and he was shocked, so shocked that he offered me a substantial raise if I would stay. I wavered only for a moment because I knew in my heart that this was my chance to have a new career and a better life." He was fortunate in being offered a position with a firm in the new field of advertising. And since this occurred within a week of his departure from the other company, he did not need to touch the savings.

In time he became the head of a different advertising firm, and as a successful CEO he was frequently asked to speak to groups of young men about creating a career that was rewarding personally, as well as financially. He stressed as the most important principle—find something that you love to do, and then ask yourself how you can create that career for yourself. He then told his own story of sacrificing in order to save money for the transition.

He described the learning from that experience in these words,

"That cushion of money meant that I would never have to feel trapped in a job again. If I didn't like the job I could walk out at any time. Somehow this self-assurance was understood by my new boss without ever putting it into words. I was treated with respect, and I enjoyed working to make the company a success. So valuable was that money to me as psychological support that, even though I moved to several different firms and eventually founded my own company, I never touched the money. To this day, there is that same savings account with five hundred dollars, plus a great deal of accumulated interest."

That savings account gave him the permission to risk taking a second and third chance, doing the work that he loved.

Sometimes we need to experience a small taste of success before we can believe that a second chance is possible for us. Moshe Feldenkrais was a person who was a wonder worker when it came to providing such an experience. Born in Russia, and trained as a scientist with degrees in physics and engineering, he worked in Paris until 1940 when he escaped to England. After a knee injury from soccer, he began a serious study of the mechanical functioning of the body and the mind-body connection. He was able to re-train the neuro-muscular functioning of his knee and the injury was healed.

That experience led to a second career. For over forty years he offered training workshops all over the world. He developed a system called Functional Integration, which became known as the Feldenkrais Method. Essentially it was a way of teaching the mind and the body to function in new ways, by very gentle, small changes in movement. And although people called him a miracle-worker and a healer, he dismissed such comments. He said, "I am a teacher, and these people are my pupils. They discover that the body can re-learn again and again."

Even people with severe physical problems like cerebral palsy were able to improve their neuro-muscular control and functioning. And although Moshe Feldenkrais helped many celebrities and world leaders, he was happiest when he could teach a crippled child that it is possible to move in ways that are less awkward and more graceful than the child had believed possible. The laughter of such a child was Moshe's great reward.

The great legacy of Feldenkrais is his reminder to us that the body is almost infinitely capable of learning new and better ways of functioning. Thus offering us constant opportunities for second and third chances to be healthy. I have found much inspiration in his example of selfless teaching. I believe that many who know of his life story can also be inspired to want to help others have that second chance at health, whether it is physical or emotional.

A second, or third, or fourth chance is always available to us. Life is endlessly creative. Only our fear narrows our vision and deludes us into believing that new opportunities are not available to us. The previous examples serve to remind us that the future can be different from the past.

The inspiring stories of a young man from Vietnam, a widow and her daughter, a trapped office worker, and a man who learned to heal an injured knee awaken us to the reality of second chances that await us all. In addition, one of the side effects of the gifts of new opportunities given these people was a desire to share their inspiration with others. Having known the joy of experiencing a second chance in life, they wanted to make similar opportunities available to others.

As the saying goes: ***If at first you don't succeed, try, try again.*** Grab the brass ring. If you can't or don't catch it at first, be assured that the universe will give you another try at it. Get ready for the next time around. **Reach out and grasp the brass ring, and know that this can be the fulfillment of a life-long dream.**

CHAPTER TEN

Uncovering the Treasure

In the Prefecture of Shizuoka in Japan, there is a remarkable institution. It is called Nemunoki Gakuen, or Silk Tree School. Founded by an actress named Mariko Miyagi, the school is also home to a group of handicapped children. As reported by Robert Hollis, in an interview published in the Honolulu Advertiser, the school has become famous internationally. Many of the children have severe physical disabilities and suffer from autism, epilepsy and cerebral palsy. Until recently in Japan such children were hidden away out of a sense of shame.

Mariko Miyagi has helped to change those attitudes. While others saw only the infirmity and handicap, she looked for the inner gifts and talents and helped to uncover the hidden treasure of each child. She discovered that these children had amazing powers of concentration and she encouraged them to spend some time each day drawing and painting.

Today the works of these children are shown around the world, and their sales help to support the school. Miyagi has said that the sale of their art has given the students a sense of self-worth that is invaluable. But their success has also altered public attitudes about handicapped children, since now many are viewed, not as inferior, but as children with physical disabilities who are also creative geniuses. Undoubtedly much of the accomplishment has been fostered by the love and affection lavished by Mariko Miyagi, who makes her home with these children.

Over the years I have been impressed by the almost miraculous effects of such caring in enabling adults, as well as children, to discover and embrace talents that lay hidden for years. The effects touch not only the person who uncovers the inner treasure, but also the caring person who encouraged and supported the search.

I remember a gifted woman who was director of a city-sponsored recreation center in Los Angeles. She had a wonderful ability to sense what talents needed to be revealed in the children who flocked to her center. She paired up a shy young girl with a very outgoing girl, and taught them a dance for a later recital. The confident steps of the one girl allowed the shy child to move more freely until she was able to dance with equal grace. For others, the director encouraged sculpting, painting or drama, being more a supportive guide than a formal teacher. She even enabled me to surprise myself as I molded and etched a pewter plate as a gift for my mother. I would not have thought I possessed such artistic ability.

In later years I spoke to this woman who had long since retired from active work. I asked her what had been the most rewarding part of her long career. Without hesitation she replied, "Oh, the joy of seeing children come alive with the discovery of new talents and creativity."

A special kind of creative gift can appear in people whom we may judge to be unlikely possessors of such talent. I remember joining a choral group at a bank where I worked as a young man. I was surprised to see that a rather shy man, who also seemed rather dour, had joined. The music director recognized this man's hidden talent, and asked if he could offer my colleague a few practical suggestions for voice projection and breathing. The shy man agreed and they worked together privately for several sessions. None of the other choral members attached much significance to this until our first public performance.

Suddenly, in a brief baritone solo this shy, dour man's voice soared to the final note much to our astonishment. His rather thin voice had taken on warmth and timbre and was beautiful. Not surprisingly, his personality also began to take on more warmth, as he rejoiced with the discovery of this hidden talent, and accepted the praise and recognition of his co-workers.

There is an echo of this unlikely discovery in a story told by Max De Pree, son of the founder of Herman Miller, Inc., a furniture factory famous for its innovative management practices.

In the early years of the company, the millwright had a very important job, overseeing the operation of the power system. This particular millwright died and the founder felt it appropriate to visit the man's family. During his visit the widow asked if she could read some poetry, and when she finished, Mr. De Pree said that the poetry was beautiful and asked who wrote it. The woman said that her husband, the millwright, was the poet.

De Pree was astonished, and reflecting on this unknown gift of one of his workers, he wondered: Was this man a poet who did millwright's work, or was he a millwright who wrote poetry? And out of this reflection came the realization that all of his workers undoubtedly had a diversity of talents and, as a manager and leader, he wanted to help them to uncover and utilize these hidden gifts. His company became a model for its management style, and has been listed in *Fortune* magazine as sixth in excellence of management in the entire country.

The effectiveness of uncovering hidden talents is due in part to the simple joy of discovery, the delight in the recognition of success, of "I can," and the awareness of being enriched abundantly. In Hawaii there is a man who accomplishes this with marvelous grace. Takao Fujitani teaches judo for young children, volunteering his time twice a week. He sees judo as a way of building character, discipline and respect. He says proudly that in his 20 years of teaching, the boys who stayed in judo did not get into trouble. And his method, while strict, is aimed at building the confidence of children in their ability to master the art.

One story tells of a time when a small boy was trying to throw him. But the boy got pinned to the mat by Fujitani. He struggled to get loose and finally said, "I cannot." Fujitani relaxed his hold a bit and said to the boy in a loud voice, "You can!" , and the boy tossed him to the mat. The struggle, the extra effort and the added encouragement, pushed the boy to a new sense of strength and power, and a real joy in his accomplishment.

It is not uncommon that one child in a family will be overshadowed by an older brother or sister. Comparisons are often made which carry the message,

"Why aren't you like him, or her?" This simply makes the younger child feel inferior. How much better if parents or teachers would seek to discover the unique gifts of the younger child. The particular gift is not as important as the recognition of each child's special talents and the encouragement to give expression to those inner treasures. Exposing children to a variety of creative arts and interests can develop an initial hobby into a talent that can offer a lifetime of satisfaction.

A young man I know envied his older brother who at an early age showed a remarkable talent as an artist. A teacher discovered that the younger boy loved to listen to the stories she would read at the beginning of the afternoon class. She found that he had memorized each day's readings and would run home after school to share the story with his younger siblings. She gave him projects which demanded research with old *National Geographic* magazines. He found a bookstore that sold these for a few cents and used pictures from these magazines to illustrate his accounts of life among various primitive tribes.

It was the beginning of what would become his career as a historian of peoples in the Pacific Ocean islands. His presentations became famous for his ability to tell fascinating tales about the cultures he had studied. Both brothers now remember with affection the teacher who encouraged them to travel different roads to creative expression.

Jacques D'Amboise, a former dancer with the famed New York City Ballet, tells of a teacher who helped him to discover his talent for dancing. When he was seven years old he was forced to watch his sister's ballet classes. It was a way of keeping him away from street gangs.

Bored, he would sit and try to disrupt the class with noises.

The wise teacher ignored his antics until the end of class when the students did the big jumps. Then she challenged him to join, saying, "All right, see if you can jump as high as the girls." He jumped and loved it, feeling as if he were flying in the air. The teacher said that he could do the jumps at each class as long as he was quiet. After a few classes she said to him, "You jump high and land beautifully but you look awful in the air. You have to take the rest of the class and learn how to handle your hands and arms." And he was hooked.

D'Amboise studied with her until she sent him to George Balanchine's School of American Ballet. After a career that lasted four decades, he formed the National Dance Institute and has taught thousands of other city children. He says,

> *"Each time I can use dance to help a child discover that he can control the way he moves, I am filled with joy. He can then learn to take control of his life. If I can open the door to show a child that that is possible, it is wonderful."*

Most of these children did not go on to careers in the field of dance, but the discoveries they made for themselves were gifts that could never be taken from them.

As a teacher I have at times been surprised to hear from former students telling me of a story, or sometimes a phrase, that had a powerful impact on their lives. At the time I had no intention of offering anything so dramatic, but it happened that the student was searching for inspiration or support and my words seemed to respond to their need of the moment. One student wrote to thank me for the story concerning the Senoi tribe in Malaysia, who teach their children life values by examining their dreams.

The incident I related concerned a child who reported that he had dreamed of a tiger and was frightened. He was told that tigers in dreams have no power to harm, and that the next time he dreamed of a tiger, he should turn and face the tiger. Some days later he reported, "I dreamed of a tiger, and I faced the tiger, and the tiger ran away."

My former student said that she had experienced a severe depression, and had contemplated ending her life. But she prayed for a sign that would awaken the hope of finding a way out of the dark tunnel of anguish. She then recalled the phrase, "Face the tiger!" That night she dreamed of a tiger, and though terrified, she faced the tiger. In her own words she tells of the result, "The tiger readied himself to attack. I held my ground. As he sprung I extended my arms. The tiger vanished. In his place lilies appeared."

Such a seemingly small phrase, yet it was buried and held as a treasure until the time when its discovery would allow power to flow into the life of a woman in pain. Her crisis was over, and though her problems were many, she had discovered an inner source of strength enabling her to confront the problems and work toward finding more creative solutions for them.

One of the most moving examples of uncovering hidden treasure is shown in a small documentary film, *Looking For Me.* It depicts the work of a dance therapist, Janet Adler, in sessions with autistic children. Using a technique called mirroring, Adler would imitate the behavior of the children, gradually moving closer to them. Her patience and caring are shown in the way she respects the children's need for greater and lesser degrees of closeness.

In one segment she is working with two little girls and as one child tentatively permits her to come closer you sense the drama. Then the child moves away, her fear still too great to risk greater closeness. Back and forth the child goes, tentatively edging closer each time. Finally, at some distance away the child stops, looks up at Adler appraisingly and makes her decision. She turns and runs into the arms of Adler. It is an exquisite moment of joy heightened by the realization of how long this little girl had been imprisoned and isolated from the experience of human affection. There can be no greater discovery than that of knowing what it is to love and to be loved.

The discovery of hidden talents can also occur late in life. In Hawaii I have met a number of men and women who are retired and who have found that their volunteer work has brought new experiences, as well as new meaning, to their lives. Most of them retired from jobs that gave them security but little else. One man said, "Well, it was a job. But I wouldn't say it was rewarding."

Then, describing his volunteer work he said, "I love it. I look forward each day to the thought of being able to help someone in need. My pay for this is the gratitude of the people I assist." This group has been formed to help older men and women living in apartments in the Waikiki area. The volunteers accompany them to the store and bank, to the doctors, or they shop and cook for them. Sometimes they spend an afternoon visiting or playing cards, or even reading to those whose sight is failing. They arrange pot-luck luncheons and outings where people from the same area can get to know one another, and the project has been very successful.

One of the wonderful results has been the fact that they have given new life to many of these people who had become virtual prisoners in their own homes. And in addition, many of the people helped have discovered that they in turn possess talents that can be shared with others to bring joy to hearts grown weary of life. They send cards and gifts of homemade cookies to one another. They teach knitting and other crafts. They arrange parties where they play the piano or the guitar and sing together, finding delight in their ability to entertain each other. The many discoveries of hidden talents have brought joy to both the helpers and the helped, especially the joy of feeling needed and loved.

The search for hidden treasure has always captivated the hearts of adventurous souls. Taking part in the search for uncovering the hidden talents and unique gifts of individuals can be the most exciting and rewarding of all. In the process of the search, we are actually feeding one another, nourishing our own as well as the souls of those joining us in the search.

The beauty of this experience has never been expressed better than the words of the poet, who describes the knight who feeds a stranger and hears the voice of God saying, **"He who feeds another feeds three: himself, his hungering brother, and Me."**

CHAPTER ELEVEN

I Don't Have to Do It

The age-old, universal struggle between parent and child centers around the concepts of obedience and responsibility. The child is expected to obey and assume responsibility for his actions. This is the attitude of the parent. The child, however, enjoys neither being told what to do, nor the responsibility of doing things according to the will of the parent. One child said it well, "Every time you tell me 'I gotta', something in me says, 'I'm not gonna.'"

The reaction of this little boy is not restricted to children. Men and women in counseling will react in a similar way to demands and threats of their partners. "You have to help me more around the house." Or, "You have to tell your mother to mind her own business." And when the reaction sets in, the partners begin to hurl blame and guilt at one another.

The sadness of this situation is that when we experience this struggle over our individual "oughts," we end up with a distorted notion of responsibility. We see it only as a burdensome obligation. We think of it only in a negative way. The truth is that responsibility has another face, beautiful, positive, an expression of our finest qualities of character—honesty, integrity, courage.

In its purest sense, responsibility means that we make a conscious choice to act in a certain way. Rather than feeling that we "have to," we can say "I choose to." We move away from the resentment of being ordered about, and replace it with feelings of genuine satisfaction at being able to make a mature response to a given situation. For that is what the word denotes—the ability to respond.

I have often felt that we all would have been better served by our parents if we had been taught as children to view responsibility in a positive light. Think how differently we would feel if our parents had chosen to reward us with praise for our actions and hugs for our generous responses, rather than blame for our behavior and guilt for our reactions. How much better for us if they had said, "Who is the one responsible for cleaning up this room?", or "You have done a beautiful job all by yourself." Praise and expressions of gratitude work wonders with us, whether child or adult. They tend to encourage us to want to act responsibly.

I love the story of a friend who told me about discovering the value of this approach with her daughter. The young girl was rather frail due to a serious respiratory ailment, and as a result her mother excused her from the usual household chores. One day an emergency arose. Another child was injured during a game at school, and the mother had to take him to the hospital immediately for treatment. Reluctantly, she said to her daughter, "Honey, I hate to ask you to do this. If you don't feel well enough, it's O.K., but I have this batch of cookies ready to go in the oven. And when they are done, could you please put the roast in the oven so it will be done by dinner time?" The daughter said that she could do it.

When the mother returned a couple of hours later, she was astonished at what she found. The cookies had been baked and the remainder of the dough put away. The roast was cooking, along with vegetables and potatoes that had been peeled. The dishes were washed and the sink and counter were spotless. And the daughter was in the living room, reading a book. When asked if all the work had been too tiring for her, the daughter replied, "No, it was actually fun. I knew you would be tired when you got home, so I wanted to do something to help. I just paced myself and it was easy."

Now grown, the daughter said that the experience of being invited and challenged to offer a generous gift of herself may well have been part of the physical healing she was later to experience. And certainly, she says, it was the beginning of seeing responsibility in a new way. She now values such challenges as opportunities to demonstrate her generosity or her courage.

Choosing to respond to a challenge often enables us to tap into hidden resources of energy and strength. We seem to be able to summon unusual inner power under the pressure of a family crisis or tragedy. But the fact is that this power has been present and available to us for quite some time. We have simply not known how to access it.

A crisis forces us to respond responsibly, to act rather than merely think about acting, much like a stage actor who needs to be pushed onstage to perform. Once before the footlights and an audience, his professionalism will enable him to choose to go on with his rehearsed performance. The value of this experience is that once we realize we can perform while afraid, we gain greater confidence to repeat the successful experience.

Acting responsibly becomes easier when we learn that we can act even when we don't particularly feel like acting. Liking and enjoyment do not have to be connected with doing what needs to be done. Once I asked a young bodybuilder if his workouts were difficult and sometimes painful. He said that indeed they often were. I then asked if he enjoyed them and he replied, "No, I don't enjoy them. They are hard work, and sometimes I have to push myself to go to the gym. But what I do enjoy is the result."

This young man has understood a very important lesson. Feelings do not have to control us. We can choose to do something at the same time that our feelings are suggesting non-action. Reminding ourselves of this fact enables us to overcome inertia, to avoid finding excuses for not acting, and makes it possible to overcome obstacles. The result is satisfaction in achievement that has a powerful impact on us, in body, mind and spirit.

Fritz Perls liked to stress two words as essential for personal growth—awareness and responsibility. He believed that we must become aware of our attitudes, beliefs, thoughts and feelings. Once aware, we make choices.

We can choose to deny the reality, to avoid taking action, or we can accept ourselves as we are and choose to change those things needed for growth. This is the response where we take responsibility. For change occurs only when we take action, not merely by thinking about change.

There may be times when we need to be reminded of the hidden power we possess. A client once responded to a question by saying, "I don't think I can do that." I said, "Are you sure you cannot?" And he then said, "Well I could only do it with great difficulty."

My next question helped to trigger an important awareness in him. "Can you give yourself permission to do it with difficulty?" He laughed as he recognized he was seeking an excuse to avoid doing something he needed to do, but which he would not enjoy doing. He chose to act, even with difficulty, and experienced not only satisfaction with the result, but increased awareness of his ability to confront challenging situations.

Choosing to act, rather than having to act, brings an added gift to us. It activates the finest virtues within us. We become more sensitive to the needs of others. We more willingly reach out to help others, even at times denying ourselves something. We take the lead rather than wait for others to do so, and in the process discover that there is a joy in giving which far outweighs the small things we may give up.

This is the trademark of greatness, of heroic men and women. In all times and cultures there are legends of generous, brave people who are honored for their courageous action. From the child in Holland who put his finger in the dike, to Joan of Arc, to St. Vincent de Paul who started the first hospitals, to Gandhi and Martin Luther King, we find countless examples of heroic figures who saw what needed to be done and chose to respond generously.

Nor is this ability only given to heroic historical figures. Weekly, in the media, we see or read stories of men and women whose lives are also inspirations for us. We are touched by the example of a young boy, dying with AIDS, rejected by his schoolmates and forced to move to another community. Yet this boy held no bitterness in his heart, and chose to face his illness and death with great courage and strength.

A young couple adopts some orphaned Vietnamese children, and makes it possible for others to do the same. Young men and women still volunteer their services in programs like the Peace Corps, putting up with great inconvenience, to offer help and hope to impoverished nations. Even if they bring little in the way of modern technology, their caring and generosity is recognized and treasured by the people they touch.

There is an elementary school near my home on Hawaii, and I never fail to be impressed with the older high school students who volunteer for the school sessions with the children. They coach the children in sports. They teach the children crafts. They share interests in gardening, astronomy, and music. They learn to help the slower and shy children to discover their own unique talents, and encourage others to increase and expand their abilities. In return, they are rewarded with the gratitude and affection of the children and the awareness that they have, in some small way, helped those children to develop similar qualities of honesty and generosity. They too are heroic in their own way, just as we are when we choose to act in a responsible way, rather than feel victimized by an obligation to act.

There is a wonderful sense of liberation that comes to us as we release feelings of being made victims by the "oughts" of others. We discover that the things that happen to us are not as important as the way we choose to view these happenings. Feelings of victimization are the result of our perception, of the things we tell ourselves about what happens to us. And these are feelings that can change as we alter our judgments. In other words we are not at the mercy of our feelings, but rather in charge of them.

I remember two sisters who were estranged for twenty years, each nursing her wounded feelings. Then one sister had a stroke and was near death. Her sister rushed to her bedside in the hospital and was moved to tears at the sight of her semi-paralyzed sister. Gone was the resentment, replaced by the love that had been hidden under the hurt. In a moment in time this woman released her injured feelings and felt free to express openly her genuine love for her sister.

This kind of liberation can be ours when we choose to move beyond our self-imposed limitations of having to respond to the "oughts" of others. It can be the experience of a small triumph when we can say, **"Of course, it is not because I ought to do it, it is because I choose to do it."**

CHAPTER TWELVE

Turning Points

The Manhattan apartment was cluttered and dirty. Odd pieces of clothing had been cast about the living room, along with empty whisky bottles and cartons of partially-eaten food. Mid-morning sunlight revealed thick dust on the coffee table and stains on the carpet. A man sprawled in a large chair was struggling to listen to his visitor. Drinking had cost him his marriage and a promising career as a radio announcer. Filled with self-pity and feeling hopeless, he had retreated to his apartment and alcohol as a way of numbing the fierce inner pain. His visitor, a recovering alcoholic, had been urged by a friend to see him.

The meeting would prove to be a major turning point in the life of the radio announcer. After several minutes of conversation he rose unsteadily and said, "I appreciate your coming to visit me, but I can't follow what you are saying. I need to rest. Come back some other time." With that he made his way to the bedroom, threw himself on the unmade bed, and fell into a deep sleep.

Many hours later he awoke, dimly aware that it was night. Intending to start drinking again, he arose and headed toward the kitchen. But as he passed by the living room, a voice from the darkness spoke words that changed his life forever, "Walter, I thought you might need me, so I waited." Only then did he discover that thirteen hours had elapsed from the time he bade farewell to his visitor. Thirteen hours! The awareness of the caring and generosity behind that gesture touched him with tremendous effect. He sat down and wept tears of gratitude for the gift of this stranger who had saved him from self-destruction.

The drinker was Walter O'Keefe, a well-known radio voice for many years. This experience, which he loved to share in lectures and counseling with alcoholics, was not only the beginning of a new life of sobriety, it was the introduction to a new career. He became an ambassador of caring, going where he was invited. He used that wonderful voice and his Irish charm in the healing work of ministering to men and women struggling with alcohol addiction. As the stranger had done for him, so he too was willing to spend untold hours with people in need.

Perhaps Walter's finest work was done with alcoholic priests. A devout Catholic, he was well aware that the problem for priests was especially difficult and had to be treated with great delicacy. His wit and genuine caring earned the trust of priests, and he was able to bring many of these men to a new sense of self-confidence and commitment. Countless priests are functioning today as a result of his dedication and compassion.

Looking back upon his life in later years, Walter said to me, "I feel that my radio career was just an 'opening act' for my real life work, that of helping priests to find the path to sobriety."

An interesting note about turning points is the fact that many of them occur as a result of some painful experience or apparent tragedy. Only in retrospect do we perceive the suffering and anxiety as part of a process, a movement to new attitudes, values and life experiences.

For many great figures, imprisonment was the environment which fostered turning points in their lives. Jeremiah in biblical times, and more recently Gandhi, Viktor Frankl and Nelson Mandela. In each instance, the prison experience promoted a period of self-reflection and re-evaluation.

Jeremiah accepted his call to be a prophet for Israel. Gandhi saw that his path for the future was to be a way of non-violence. Frankl, while imprisoned in a Nazi concentration camp, saw a light in a distant farmhouse and his faith in ultimate survival was joined to his sense of mission towards his fellow prisoners. Frankl was inspired to help people find a sense of meaning in their lives. Mandela solidified his belief that one day he would help lead his people to freedom.

For some the prison experience was shattering and despairing. For the above men, it was a turning point that was a rebirth and beginning of a greater career.

A turning point is an invitation to change, which carries a powerful energy towards choosing new directions in life. The events that trigger this experience seem to be quite varied, yet one common element is an emotional reaction to one's environment. James Michener describes his own experience after escaping from a near-crash on a small South Pacific island airstrip.

> *"For some hours I walked back and forth on that Tontouta strip...to calm my nerves. But as I did I began to think about my future life and to face certain problems. I asked myself, What do I want to do with the*

remainder of my life? What do I stand for? What do I hope to accomplish with the years that will be allowed me? ...

As the stars came out and I could see the low mountains I had escaped I swore, I'm going to concentrate my life on the biggest ideals and ideas I can handle. I'm going to associate myself with people who know more than I do. And in the nearly fifty years since that night, I have steadfastly borne testimony to all my deeply held beliefs."

Michener also came to realize that thousands of other men in the South Pacific were asking themselves similar questions during night watches on ships and airstrips. Alone with their thoughts on starry nights, and aware of the dangers of wartime, many found themselves choosing new careers based on different life values.

My own experience affirms this fact. I can still recall, as clearly as if it were yesterday, standing on the shore of Guadalcanal late one evening. The air was cooled by a light breeze, and moonlight made dancing patterns on the sea. Orion was in the sky above me and I was touched by the beauty of the night making the ugliness of war fade into the background. Suddenly I became aware of an inner voice that told me my life was to be dedicated in some way to the task of helping people. I later pushed these thoughts away when I returned from the war, but they surfaced again in a few years when I felt impelled to begin studies for the priesthood. Later I would follow the path of counseling, which has remained my life career to this day.

And even now, on starry nights when the winds are balmy, I can re-experience the joy of that turning point in my life.

I was reminded of that important event many years later. Once again I was far from home, aboard a Navy ship in the China Seas. I had accepted an invitation to teach a course for Navy personnel for a period of one month. During the afternoon rest period, I would often find a shaded area on the deck in the hope of catching a breath of cooling air while I read a book.

A young sailor was standing watch nearby and he invited me to observe a huge school of sharks following the ship. We began to talk and over the period of a week he opened his heart to me. His was a tragic tale of childhood abuse, some involvement with drugs, expulsion from school, dissatisfaction with his navy experience, and rejection by his girlfriend. But it was his terrible loneliness that was his greatest burden, leading him to thoughts of suicide.

In the mysterious workings of the universe, I happened to meet him on that deck and became someone he could trust to share his burden. Gradually his mood began to change, to lighten with shared laughter and the description of my own foibles. Somehow he was able to change his focus and feel some stirrings of hope for the future. When I left the ship a few weeks later, he came to my quarters, embraced and thanked me saying, "I will never forget those talks we had. They helped me turn my life around; in fact they saved my life."

I was humbled by his expression of gratitude, and struck by the connection between this young man's turning point and my own on that night in the South Pacific many years before. It was like the fulfillment of a prophecy. Both experiences, the sailor's and my own, shared a common feeling of being touched emotionally. He responded to the genuine caring of another person, and I was moved by the sheer beauty of that tropical night. The emotional impact seemed to open not only our hearts, but also enabled us to look to the future with new faith and hope.

I have witnessed similar dramatic changes in encounter groups. One young man in a drug recovery program was troubled that he may have simply exchanged dependencies. Although he was free of drugs, he felt that he was not free to leave the program and make a new life for himself apart from the program. In a role-playing session with an older woman he re-enacted some of his earlier problems with his mother. The result of this was a kind of emotional breakthrough in which he experienced his mother as genuinely loving and caring, but over-burdened by her own problems.

His anger turned to compassion and he felt renewed and empowered by the session. He said, "I feel so full of happiness. I know now that I don't need drugs to be 'high' and I don't need the program to save my life. I just need to have loving people like you to help me from time to time." This was indeed a turning point for him. Within a few months he began a new career, and within a year he had married a girl who shared his dreams and supported him with her own inner strength.

These are examples of major turning points, significant for their drama and power. But I have discovered that most of us also have a series of smaller turning points, equally important for our lives but which arrive with less dramatic entrance. These are the experiences that encourage us to alter our direction, or attitude, at a vital moment in our lives.

One man told of his experience at his first job, that of a bank teller. The job was interesting if not challenging, and the pay was rather minimal, but he had hoped to work his way up the banking ladder. However, one morning when he arrived for work, he had an insight that became a small but significant turning point for him. Something prompted him to take a second look at his department head. He said, "I saw a man of forty-five who looked as if he was sixty. He always wore a gray suit. He had graying hair, a kind of gray complexion, and I realized he had a gray personality too. There seemed to be no joy in his life.

Suddenly I realized that I could become that man if I stayed in that deadening environment. I quit the next month and got a job in sales that started me on a series of career changes that brought me new risks, but exciting rewards as well."

I recall an incident during a family therapy session which proved to be a turning point for the mother of a teenage daughter. In the midst of a familiar argument about doing household chores, the mother complained that the daughter was negligent and had to be told constantly to wash the dishes or set the table. The mother's voice was edged with anger.

The daughter suddenly burst into tears and said, "O.K., so I don't always do things when I am told, but that still doesn't make me a bad person." The depth of her anguish was obvious to everyone, and fortunately the mother heard and understood her daughter's pain. Very gently, the mother replied, "Of course it doesn't, and I am sorry I implied that. I realize that I have been nagging you, and I intend to stop that because when I nag you, my love for you gets lost. And I don't ever want that to happen in the future."

Later the mother acknowledged that the interaction proved to be an eye opener for her, enabling her to establish a new relationship with her daughter. Her comment on the impact of her changed attitude was, "I found myself looking at my daughter through the eyes of a loving mother rather than a stern taskmaster. It was a wonderful experience that affected my relationship with others including my husband." This was a small, but important, turning point for this woman.

Recently the concept of performing random acts of kindness has swept the country with positive effects. In a number of instances, men and women have described the ways in which they experienced receiving small unexpected gestures of kindness. Some said that they were prompted to pass along similar acts of kindness. Others have suggested a more significant impact. They said that the shock or surprise of being the beneficiary of such unusual generosity made them re-examine their own lives and values.

For many it became a turning point, a new way of seeing and relating to people. In Hawaii I often take an early morning walk along a canal promenade. One day I noticed a woman picking up litter, which she put into a large plastic trash bag. I spoke to her and thanked her for her thoughtfulness. She then told me,

> *"You know I started this because I walk my dog every morning and needed to dispose of his droppings. Then I decided to pick up a few pieces of trash, and the next thing I knew, I was involved in a daily project. I*

laugh now when I think back and realize I was not very happy to have to get up early and walk my dog. But once out in the fresh air I felt energized, and now I have found that the exercise involved in picking up litter has helped my arthritis. It has been a blessing in disguise and I look forward to it every day."

Her example became a turning point for other walkers. Now there are six or seven men and women with trash bags picking up litter, not only along the canal but in the surrounding neighborhood as well.

A turning point can also be the result of a new interest or skill. A fourth grade teacher opened up the world of astronomy for me, as well as an interest in nature. I would search the skies at night for a glimpse of Cassiopeia's Chair or the North Star and the Big Dipper. And I would gather wildflowers so that I could research them in the teacher's wonderful encyclopedia. I have carried both interests with me around the world, comforted by familiar night skies, and delighted with the discovery of new and exotic flowers and plants. These two interests were gifts of a dedicated woman who was committed to expanding the minds of her students.

A gourmet cook told of the incident that became a turning point for her. Her mother ran a small hotel, and as a child she loved to watch her mother knead bread and make pies. She was nine years old when one morning her mother, ill with the flu, said that she would have to omit desserts from the menu for that day. Her daughter astonished her by saying, "I can make a cake and some pies. I know how." The result was that the daughter gradually took charge of the kitchen and started on a career that made her famous and gave her much personal satisfaction.

Perhaps the most significant turning points are those which affect the way we relate to another person. Some event or experience will alter the way we view a person, and will change the way we feel. I remember having dinner with an officer and his wife on the east coast, where I was conducting a course for the Marines. Their three year old daughter had been put to bed.

During the meal her father said that he and his wife were very concerned about the nightmares the child was experiencing. Since he was a pilot, he would be away from home at regular intervals, and the child's nightmares seemed to be worse at those times. I suggested that the father spend more time with the child, that he put her to bed when he was at home, reading to her until she fell asleep and that he be the one to respond to her if she awakened in fright.

One night when she awoke screaming, he held and comforted her. As the little girl told of her fears, he realized that somehow she had connected his flying with an incident from television, and she feared he would never return. Gradually, as he spent more time with her, the fear disappeared. But for the father it was a powerful turning point. The preciousness of this child, her need for greater affection and attention, changed his view from an officer who had a wife and child, to a father whose love and devotion were essential to the growth of this child so dear to his heart.

As these examples show, the triggering mechanism for a turning point can come from a variety of sources: a personal crisis; imprisonment; the experience of natural beauty amidst pain or suffering; sharing one's burden with a caring person; a sudden insight into a familiar situation; the example of another person's generosity or sacrifice; the discovery of a new interest or skill; and the experience of seeing a loved one through eyes informed by a fresh vision of caring and compassion. The condition for this remarkable change seems to be a willingness to open our hearts and a readiness to respond to new challenges.

A turning point, once embraced, is actually a miracle of grace that brings us new life and rewarding accomplishments. **A turning point occurs when we stop using life's challenges as stumbling blocks and we change them into stepping stones.**

CHAPTER THIRTEEN

Living With Mystery

I had occasion last year to spend a morning with a group of third-graders, and it was a great learning experience for me. I asked them to tell me of the things in the world of nature that posed questions for them. Some of their replies were: "What makes the sun go down and come up?" "Why is the sky blue?," "Where do the birds go when they are ready to die?" "Why is it hot in one place and cold in another" "How does the moon make tides?" and "How do the plovers know the way to Hawaii and back to Alaska?" (The latter concerns a phenomenon that amazes us adults as well as children, who observe the annual ritual here in Hawaii.) I was struck by the fact that the questions seemed to arise not from scientific curiosity but rather from a sense of wonder in the face of mystery.

Unfortunately, as many of these children get older, they will no longer maintain their curiosity about such phenomena, and they may well find their sense of wonder dimmed. All too often parents and adult teachers may discourage their attempts to find answers for puzzling observances. It is unfortunate because when they become adults they will be handicapped in their ability to relate to mystery, which exists in many forms during our life journey.

It is sad for another reason. Stifling a child's curiosity often inhibits the use of their imagination, which is the source of creativity, and the wellspring of invention and discovery. This repression occurs not only in the field of science, but in many areas of the child's artistic expression.

One of the rewarding experiences in counseling is helping clients to stimulate the imagination, to begin to discover new ideas, options and possibilities for their lives and careers. I have often compared the experience to that of a child opening exciting new gifts at Christmas. It is the wonderful feeling of being in charge of one's life, rather than being a victim of circumstances. It is equally wonderful to witness.

However, many clients never experience this delight. They approach life's challenges as problems to be solved, rather than lessons to be learned, or as mysteries to be experienced. An inner conviction maintains they can solve problems and resolve difficulties by intellectual analysis alone. They want to understand the causes and explore the origins of their emotional distress. They seek answers to the whys and hows of their current experience, believing this will lead them to the Mecca of personal happiness and inner peace.

Of course this approach, which seems eminently sensible, ignores the fact that while they may have the curiosity of a child, they lack the open, accepting mind of a child. Philosophers from the East term this a "beginner's mind." It is characterized as a mind that is without prejudice, eager to learn, ready to accept new information, even though that information may seem to run counter to previously learned facts or theories. It is the difference between a response that says, "Well that doesn't sound like something that would work," and a response that says, "Ah! That is an entirely new way of viewing the situation."

The first response immediately questions, the second response accepts. The first response indicates a partial answer; it is a closed mind. The second response recognizes its ignorance and is thus an open mind. I experienced the difference between these two attitudes a few years ago when I was conducting workshops for organizations in the United States and Japan as a management consultant. Some of these were aimed at reducing the conflict within an organization.

One of the challenges for me was the fact that the workshops in the United States were ordered by top management. The workers had no voice in the decision and came to the workshops with their resentment apparent to everyone. Their minds were closed by their resistance to the process. With a great deal of luck and some creative trust-building, it was possible to overcome this resistance in some cases. But the effort was time consuming and left little opportunity for more creative problem-solving.

During the same period I was invited to do some training with executives from large Japanese companies. We met at a secluded resort in a mountain area, and I was joined by a Japanese-speaking trainer. There were only twelve men in this group, and we formed a circle of chairs in a rather bare meeting room of a rustic hotel. I was struck by the respect they offered me, and the readiness to learn, as well as by their ability to accept some painful truths about themselves.

One evening after the day's work had ended I met with my co-trainer and shared my surprise at their attitudes. I said, "These are very important and powerful men in their companies, yet in this workshop they are as humble and open as young schoolboys." My friend replied, "Oh, but you see this is different. In their companies they know how to run the administrative aspects very well, but they recognize that they don't possess some of the new communication skills and they want to learn. Besides, it has always been our tradition to show respect to our teachers because we believe they have great gifts for us."

For me it was a revelation, a first hand experience of well-educated men, willing to approach problems with an open mind. Later I was able to follow up with interviews and was not surprised to discover how well they had integrated the material and translated it into their companies with great effectiveness.

An open, or "beginner's mind," is not one that believes everything it hears. But it does receive the information without immediately evaluating it in light of previous information. When we function with an open mind, we accept the information and are willing to examine it in more detail, to get more data so that we have a fuller picture of the meaning of the information.

I remember my mentor Carl Rogers doing this during meetings with his colleagues when they would give him negative feedback. Someone might say, "Carl, I think that idea is crazy. It will never work." And Carl would respond without irritation and say, "Well, it may be a nutty idea. Tell me why you think it is crazy and why it won't work."

At the time I would feel some irritation for what I perceived as an indirect attack upon his judgment. And more than once I heard Carl reply to the reasons given by saying, "You know, I believe you are right. Viewed from that perspective I think it is a dumb idea, and it won't work."

Carl accepted the information given him, and was willing to wait and surround that information with additional data that enabled him to alter his original opinion. Not only was this an example of an open mind at work, it was also a model for responding to someone who is criticizing you. Both were valuable lessons for me.

One of the disadvantages of a closed mind is that we get locked into a fruitless search for answers. The closed mind works like a computer program. It knows only the information stored, and rejects the possibility of new data. It is what some term "left-brain thinking," using rational and intellectual approaches to problems. "Right-brain thinking" taps into our imagination and intuition, which offer creative ways of examining old issues. Furthermore, our emotional energy gets drained by the frustrating process of going over the same old material in the same old ways.

Virginia Satir, the founder of Family Therapy, once said that rather than attempt to get people to view their problems from new perspectives she chose another approach. She might ask the father and his son, for instance, to change their physical positions. She would ask the father to kneel on the floor and the son to stand on a chair and have them talk to one another.

The experiment produced a number of reactions. The father might say, "I felt intimidated by his height." And the son might say, "I felt strong for a change." In some cases this led to laughter and above all, a change in the energy of the participants. The energy was no longer locked into the problem but connected to the father and son in a new way, sharing a search for solutions rather than fighting about the problems facing them.

An open mind functions without many preconceptions. It recognizes that in life we must live with mystery. There are things that we simply cannot adequately understand or explain. Philosophies and religions offer their theories in an effort to explain what may in reality be unexplainable.

From the beginning of time, humans have sought to explain suffering, sickness and death. Even the process of healing remains a mystery. We know the body heals, but not precisely how or why it heals itself. Some mysteries are to be explored and examined, but others can only be accepted. The open mind knows this, and chooses not to waste energy on possible explanations, but to use it for new ideas and even new adventures on our life journey.

Perhaps our need to fulfill our roles in life may serve to close rather than open our minds. We see many men and women who function along these lines: parents give the orders and children obey, teachers have the answers and students have the questions. With these attitudes, it can be very difficult for individuals to admit ignorance or ask for help. There is a fear of "losing face" that prevents the growth of humility and fosters a false form of arrogance. This need to appear all-knowing and wise can be a terrible burden as well.

A client told of an incident with his teenage son which proved to be not only a valuable lesson for him, but the beginning of a new and richer relationship with his son. This man had prided himself on keeping his word to others, and on doing his work in a timely and responsible manner. He had an understanding with his son that the boy would cut the grass on the following Saturday.

The day arrived, and morning became afternoon with no sign of the grass being mowed. The father began to get angry, assuming that his son was either being disobedient or irresponsible. By late afternoon when the son returned home from playing sports, the father exploded and scolded his son severely. When he paused for breath in his tirade, the son quietly said to his father, "Hey, Dad, what's happening?" It was a genuine question, not a defensive response, and the father was taken aback.

The remark forced him to open his mind, and allowed his anger to lessen so that he could hear the explanation his son offered. The son said, "Dad, I agreed to cut the lawn, and I'm going to cut it now. I didn't tell you I would cut it in the morning. I decided to play ball in the morning and cut the lawn in the afternoon when it was cooler." And he added, "Dad, don't be mad at me if I decide to do it my way instead of your way."

The father later admitted that for a moment they had changed roles. His son was the wise and calm one, and he was acting more like an emotional child. He also saw that he had learned to do a job and then play, whereas his son found it easier to have a relaxing time first and then tackle the job. Neither way was in itself right or wrong; they were simply different approaches to a problem.

The valuable lesson for the father was that his son's approach seemed to be one that was more satisfying. His own way was marked more by a sense of obligation, and the satisfaction came from an awareness of "doing one's job." Reflection on these differing approaches helped the father to realize that much of his sense of accomplishment in life had been rather joyless. What he learned from his son was that it was possible to play and still "do one's job."

Some time later he was able to share this with his son, and today, although their lives are quite different and the son is married, their best times are "playing" together when they regularly set aside time for camping trips. In this incident, the son's gentle response enabled the father to abandon his notion that "father knows best," and accept suggestions from his son with a more open mind.

This need to appear all-wise or knowing can foster an arrogance that makes it very difficult to have an open mind. I remember a story told of Sigmund Freud discussing one of his dreams with Carl Jung. At one point Jung pressed for further details and Freud said he did not want to tell him those details. When asked why, Freud said, "Because I am afraid you will lose respect for me." And in telling the story years later, Jung said, "It was that response, rather than the details of the dream, that made me lose respect for him."

Maintaining an open mind is the secret of learning to live with mystery. We no longer have to have an understanding of everything that occurs, or a need to search continually for the underlying causes of suffering and tragedy in our lives. We are better able to be satisfied with the belief that there is a reason for these things, even though it may not be immediately available to us. We can accept in faith the things we cannot explain by reason.

In some ways it is having the open, innocent mind of a child, rather than the suspicious, questioning mind of a world-weary adult. It is a positive response to the biblical directive: "unless you become as little children you shall not enter the kingdom of heaven." In many ways, the metaphor is most apt. We are, after all, very much like little children in the face of a universe that is extremely complex and filled with mystery beyond our powers of comprehension.

One of the most striking aspects of the experience of the astronauts, after they returned to earth, was a common admission of their feelings of humility and smallness when faced with the vastness and mystery of outer space. With all their technological brilliance and scientific expertise, they were awed by the experience of viewing the universe from the distant reaches of space travel. They felt like little children again, gazing at miracles beyond their intellectual grasp. They also described the incredible sense of wonder at the majesty of the universe in which we live. The result for them was a humility and openness to new ideas and perspectives that would have a profound effect on every aspect of their later lives.

Richard Moss, in his book *How Shall I Live,* tells of a revelation in his own life that helped him to open his mind and ultimately to learn to live with mystery. He said that for many years he had fixed notions about various aspects of his life. Most of these had rigid value judgments attached. His work as a physician was challenging and absorbing, but he discovered that he was "addicted to intensity." Things that brought excitement were considered good; things that were not exciting were to be avoided. Work was great, but washing clothes was boring.

The revelation was the awareness that he needed to direct his energies towards "undoing" rather than "doing" as he had valued previously. He had to let go of these long-held ideas, and allow his rigid values to soften and change, to permit fresh air and different perspectives to inform his choices. The process was, in fact, like the beginning of a new life for him, moving him from a traditional physician into a metaphysician and healer.

The recipe for living with mystery is simple, if not easy: acquiring humility; adopting the child's sense of wonder; or the "beginner's mind," exploring mysteries that seem to contain a lesson for us; as well as accepting mysteries that we cannot understand. Some of the explorations will open up new worlds of creativity and invention, while the acceptance of others will bring inner peace to our hearts. Mystery then changes from a puzzle to be explained, to a source of wonder and beauty.

Albert Einstein said it well: **"The most beautiful thing we can experience is the mysterious. It is the source of all true art and science."**

CHAPTER FOURTEEN

Beyond the Blemish

One of the most enduring and captivating stories is that of the fairy tale, *Beauty and the Beast.* The allegory tells of a beautiful young woman who accepts the kindly ministrations of a very ugly-looking beast. She does not deny his ugly physical appearance, rather she sees beyond the externals and discovers the inner beauty of his soul and the loving expressions of his heart. Her genuine acceptance of him, her loving him without condition, enables the miracle of transformation to occur. The Beast is changed into a handsome prince before her eyes.

The allegory suggests that we too, like the young prince, may be living under a kind of spell that allows our worst qualities to dominate our public persona. Self-centeredness, arrogance, pettiness, irritability, and a host of other ugly traits may characterize our behavior. And we may be unaware of the image we are projecting. To paraphrase the words of the poet, Robert Burns, "Would that God might give us the ability to see ourselves as others see us."

Eric Berne may offer us a clue toward the elimination of our blindness. In his famous book, *Games People Play,* he describes a type of person who has little insight into himself, who is rather insecure, who seeks love but fears rejection. Not able to accept his own faults, he forms a practice of noticing the faults and failings of others.

Berne calls this negative preoccupation, "looking for the blemish." Not only have we experienced times when this has been our own way of reacting, we have met men and women who seem to be absorbed in their readiness to judge and be critical of others.

This characteristic is one of the most destructive elements in personal and professional relationships. Criticism and blaming form the substance of the most common complaints in marriage counseling. The ensuing feelings of emotional hurt that arise from this negative attack do great damage to the relationship.

Interestingly enough, I have found the same complaints from workers during management consulting sessions. Men and women told of their resentment towards managers who were quick to criticize, yet rarely offered praise. One man said, "My boss is never pleased with the quantity or the quality of my work, or if he is, I have never heard him say so. After a while you lose interest in trying to do a better job." A sad comment, for it indicates this man has given up hope, and that is a tragic way to live.

More often than not, people like this boss are unaware of their critical attitudes. It often takes a bit of counseling for them to realize that this pattern may have been modeled after critical parents or teachers.

One woman manager, who was astonished to discover that her clerks all described her as "very critical," found that she was imitating the manner of her mother. She said, "I have never been able to please that woman. She is still critical of everything I do."

Understanding the feelings of resentment coming from her clerks, she was able to abandon her constant negative judgments, and offer gratitude and praise as well as corrective remarks. The change in morale within a few months was remarkable. One of her clerks commented, "I no longer shake in my boots when I am called into her office. She is much more understanding, and willing to help us if something needs to be changed."

Counseling often helps to reveal a critical attitude, but it is possible to gain some insight by examining the way we tend to respond to people. One of the clues can be a defensiveness to what we perceive as criticism of ourselves. We usually resort to criticism in return, or blaming. But our initial response suggests that we may be quick to perceive remarks as criticism because we are habitually prone to look for things to criticize in others.

We tend to "look for the dust on the table," to search for what is wrong, or for what is awry, rather than noticing what is right and correct as well as the negative view. We need to see "beyond the blemish," to take in the whole picture. It may mean seeing the intent in the action or gesture, as a loving parent will do with the gift of a child's imperfect drawing.

The habit of looking for the blemish, and missing the larger picture, came home to me a number of years ago when I was part of a small group touring the island of Kauai in Hawaii. There were six of us who had hired a limousine for the day to see the sights. Two elderly women were the last to arrive for the trip and as the driver was explaining the beautiful scenery along the way, I was aware that the two women were carrying on a conversation of their own. It consisted mostly of critical comments about the service during breakfast, the faulty air-conditioning in the hotel, concerns over the price of souvenirs, etc. All of this while our car was driving past some of the most gorgeous views in the world.

When we returned to the hotel, we all thanked the driver and commented on what a marvelous experience it had been. I was pleasantly surprised to hear both elderly women agreeing that the sightseeing had been beautiful, and I thought perhaps I had been a bit harsh in my judgment of them along the trip. However, as they headed into the hotel, one of the women said to her friend, "Well, it was a nice trip, but it was awfully long, and we have seen pretty scenery before." They actually had missed most of the outstanding sights while conversing.

The last remark also contains a clue for us. Her, "yes, but..." can serve as a reminder for us to be aware of our own tendency to respond to a comment by saying, "yes, but..." Very often we are not actually agreeing, we are disagreeing, but the introductory, "yes" seems to soften our opposite position. That kind of response alerts us to the fact that we have been looking for something to find fault with, or which will form the basis for an objection.

The important learning for us is the awareness that this may be a common occurrence for us, and a habitual pattern we might want to change. The use of this response tends to trigger an argument, since the other party feels a need to defend his statement or opinion, and it usually ends up being non-productive, often increasing angry feelings.

People who are defensive and critical most often reveal more about themselves than they do about the things they are defending or criticizing. Frequently they are insecure and fearful, and thus they take the position that the best defense is a good offense. Their need to protect themselves in this way should awaken in us a sense of compassion, rather than anger or resentment. Like the Beast in the allegory, their external behavior can be ugly, yet they may be seeking the kind of non-judgmental and compassionate caring that will free them from their self-imposed curses.

I remember a troubled teenager who was judged by most adults to be incorrigible. He lied and cheated his way through life, and could not be trusted to do even the simplest tasks assigned to him. That is, until he met a counselor who looked beyond his blemishes.

She arranged for him to do some shopping for her. When he returned with the groceries, she took the coin purse and dumped the contents into her larger purse, without counting the change. After several times the boy said, "You didn't count the change. I could have cheated you." She said, "I know. But I don't think you did. And I would rather believe you want to be honest, so I will never count the change."

This unconditional acceptance answered a deep need in the boy. He yearned to be loved and considered trustworthy, but from childhood he had been labeled as a "bad boy, and he decided to live up to the label. The counselor's trust and caring had the opposite effect, making him want to earn that trust and acceptance. A gradual transformation took place enabling him to become a responsible adult who now serves as a counselor for other troubled youths.

I am also reminded of a German baroness who turned several of her castles into schools and training institutes after World War II. She trained young women as caregivers to assist families struggling to exist after the war. They cared for children and the elderly. They cooked and cleaned and helped to teach the children. They did whatever was needed in a particular home, and they did this without charge, believing they had a spiritual calling to care for their neighbors in need.

I visited with these young women and was impressed with their dedication and joyful spirits. When I shared my reactions the baroness said to me,

> *"When these women first walked into a home, the people said it was as if an angel from heaven had been sent to them. And their gratitude in turn made the young women feel as if they were angels from heaven. The gift of love worked miracles for the people and for the women helping them."*

The genuine expression of love, freely given without judgments, invariably touches both the person receiving it and the giver of that love.

A similar experience is that of the nuns who set up a hospital on the island of Molokai to care for the lepers there. Although the hospital has been closed and the nuns are no longer there, the memory of their caring is still very much alive. The few remaining men and women speak of the nuns with great affection and gratitude.

One man said,

> *"Everyone loved them, because they never looked upon us as outcasts from society. They were not repelled by our disfigurement. They treated us with dignity, and made us feel wanted and loved. They helped us to sing and dance, and laugh together. They were our family."*

High praise indeed for a group of women who were able, by looking past the externals, to offer the kind of love that transforms.

These examples illustrate a truth we all too often forget. Miracles of healing are not limited to the body, but touch the soul and renew the spirit of a person. We feel the love that heals and brings us to new life when we experience love by someone who: accepts us unconditionally; walks with us when our pace is slow; inspires us when we are disheartened; and supports and encourages us with affection and laughter. It is a love that sees our weakness and even our ugliness and accepts us "as is," looking beyond those qualities to the inner heart and soul, and gracing these with understanding and compassion.

I remember well the words I chose to share with the mourners who attended the funeral of my sister, killed in a tragic auto accident. I spoke of the way she had touched my life with her generosity and especially her gift of laughter. And I added, "I loved her not despite her faults and frailties, but with them because they made her the uniquely lovable person she was." Through her I learned to look beyond the blemish, and although it is a lesson that must constantly be re-learned, it is one I value highly.

Perhaps the best news is the fact that this ability to see the larger picture, to choose new responses to attacks and irritating remarks, is one that can be learned. It is not easy and requires practice, but the benefits affect us as well as the person with whom we are relating.

A high school teacher has developed a course for her students, centering around Conflict Resolution. She uses role playing situations in which she teaches students how to avoid defensive reactions. As an example, when a person is being told he is stupid to take a certain position, she will suggest an acknowledgment of the remark, "Well maybe the position is not so smart. Tell me why you think it's dumb."

Her point is to allow the person to feel that you have heard him. Next offer him understanding rather than defense. He may actually have a different perspective, which is valid. Or he may have a need to denigrate you in order to feel important. In any event, thinking of him with understanding will change the tone of your voice and the manner of your response, and will most likely have a positive effect upon the person making the attack.

Ancient myths and legends usually contain a profound truth hidden in the folds of allegory. The stories of Cinderella, Sleeping Beauty, of frogs turning into princes, of ugly ducklings being transformed into beautiful creatures, all underline the mystery of transformation. The key lies in understanding and acceptance, in selfless giving of genuine love, and then the miracle can occur. Through the wonderful alchemy of this love, people are changed and born anew. They are gifted with beauty and wondrous powers. A further message is that these incredible miracles are not merely for princes and princesses. They are available to you and me, if only we are willing to pay the small price of looking beyond the blemish to find the inner beauty of the person before us.

In the words of Antoine de St. Exupéry in *The Little Prince,* **"It is only with the heart that one can see rightly; what is essential is invisible to the eye."**

CHAPTER FIFTEEN

What Do I Do Now?

Some of my most valuable life lessons have emerged from moments when it seemed that I had run out of options. Not knowing what to do next, and feeling rather helpless, I often acted in desperation. This happened a number of times in therapy when I felt that both the client and I were stuck in a rut.

In one case I suggested we leave the office and walk to a small shelter overlooking the beach. The day was sunny, the sea was whipped by a light wind, and it felt very peaceful. We sat in silence for a while and then the man began to talk. The scene reminded him of scenes from his childhood, and he was able to release some long-held pain from those early days.

I discovered that he was not alone in his need to feel free from eyes that could judge him critically. The learning enabled me to be more sensitive to similar needs of clients, and to find other ways for them to express themselves and feel safe at the same time. However, this particular insight resulted not from a creative impulse, but rather as a spontaneous response from feeling desperate to alter an uncomfortable experience.

On another occasion I was working with a teenage boy who had a high IQ, yet was failing in school. His parents brought him for counseling and it soon became clear that he had no intention of giving me much information about himself. His responses were, "yes," "no," "I don't know," or silence while he stared out the window. In desperation I asked him if he knew how to shoot pool.

Eyeing me suspiciously he said, "Well, a little." I took him to a game room and challenged him to a match. The moment I saw the way he handled the cue and chalk, it was apparent that he had spent more than a few hours at pool tables. But he was nervous, and lost the first game. He challenged me to another, and this time his self-confidence enabled him to play very well. As he began to feel more assured of his playing, he started to talk, telling me of his anger and frustration with his parents, especially his father. When we returned to the office, he became silent again.

The following week, and for several weeks afterwards, our counseling session was held at the pool table where he was consistent in winning most of the games. Somehow the game of pool became a medium through which we could communicate with one another. I was able to discover the source of his pain and anguish, and to bring his parents to insights that helped them to see their son through different eyes. I have often been grateful for the desperation that led to a successful resolution of a serious family problem.

Incidents such as these prompted me to recall other times when I chose some form of action because I was at a loss, feeling bereft of options. And in discussing this phenomenon with friends, I found that they also had made some choices out of desperation that produced happy results. One man described his frustration with handling his little girl's temper tantrums. At his wit's end, he grabbed a clown mask and acted out the role of an outrageous circus clown. The child's angry crying turned to laughter and her father discovered a talent for acting that eventually led to stage performances which were very rewarding.

Dr. Elisabeth Kubler-Ross, the noted Swiss psychiatrist, is the author of *On Death and Dying,* which revolutionized attitudes towards terminal patients. She has described a number of her own life experiences that demonstrate the value of finding ourselves facing problems for which we do not have an immediate solution.

Dr. Kubler-Ross tells of having to flee Europe when Hitler was invading one country after another. Upon arrival in New York with her physician husband, she was unable to join the staff of hospitals because her own medical license was not recognized in the United States. Her husband's salary did not even cover the rent. What to do? In desperation she accepted a position in a state hospital working with patients labeled as hopeless, chronic schizophrenics. Yet the challenge of having to overcome the obstacles of working with these patients stimulated her to find new ways of relating to them.

Dr. Kubler-Ross helped these men and women to create new lives for themselves. She gave them hope, by providing them with the first steps toward small success experiences. She taught them how to use the subway, and how to shop. She even found them jobs. In short, she helped them to believe in themselves and in their ability to function and to survive outside the hospital. Eventually she was able to discharge 94 percent of her patients. And in reflecting on her experience, she realized that the moments when she asked, "What do I do now?" were simply brief waiting periods before a new window of opportunity would open for her.

A friend of mine describes a similar kind of learning that emerged from an experience that had felt like hitting a blank wall. His marriage had fallen apart. He was taking some teaching assignments, although he had been a successful psychotherapist. And he felt as if he had reached the "end of his rope," even toying with thoughts of suicide. He could not see any immediate hope for the future. However, a caring therapist, who was also a close friend, enabled him to hang on" until some new opportunity presented itself to him. A mutual friend told him of an opening with a governmental agency training officers for top secret work. He was accepted for the position, and became an expert in his field.

Like Kubler-Ross, he now sees that this job was a true gift from heaven, for he has a special talent that draws people to him and enables them to place their trust in him. He has been extremely successful in what he now terms "the work I was called upon to do." The "blank wall" was only a momentary obstacle over which he summoned the courage to achieve his goal.

Research shows that so many of these desperate experiences are simply tests for us, enabling us to discover hidden inner strengths and power to move our lives into new paths benefiting others as well as ourselves. Sometimes the desperation forces us to act even when we are not sure of the outcome.

An old friend told of his experience during the Depression days. With no money in his wallet and facing a "blank wall" as far as a job was concerned, he decided to visit a friend who was an editor for a popular magazine. Some inner voice told him that he would think of something to offer this man in return for a small payment. He was without any creative idea until he turned the handle of the door to his friend's office.

At that moment he had an inspiration. He pictured an entirely new format for the magazine which would appeal to a new group of readers, and even drew a quick cartoon to illustrate the idea. His friend liked the suggestion, paid him twenty-five dollars, and used the concept to turn his magazine into a successful publication. The payment was small but it fed his family, and it gave him renewed confidence in his ability as a creative writer. His own future was assured, for he was able to sell his material for many years until he retired.

There are also times when we need to do some inner spiritual work on ourselves before we can gain the momentum to move in a new direction. During an interview a man told of his desperation after a business failure and tax problems had hounded him for years. At one point he even contemplated suicide. But some inner power enabled him to hang on, to keep believing he would find a way out of his dilemma. One day he awoke from sleep and heard a voice saying very clearly, "All you have to do is forgive yourself." As described in her book, *Opening to Miracles,* Betty Clare Moffat reports that this man did as he was told. He forgave himself and everyone in his past for their mistakes. The next day he began to confront and successfully deal with his problems, one by one.

Often overcoming a false pride is the particular bit of spiritual work that is needed. We may find that it is difficult to admit that we need outside help, and that it is equally hard to ask for help. Prayer is often the first step toward admitting our neediness, and opening our hearts to ask for and receive the assistance we need to overcome our obstacle. As many men and women who have overcome their addiction to alcohol through the AA organization can attest, this first step is essential.

Tony Robbins, the motivational speaker, has helped many people by teaching them ways to overcome their belief that the "wall" is insurmountable. By means of physical exercises and a variety of activities, he proves to them that they have incredible unused power and an imagination that can move them beyond the "wall." Satisfied students from his seminars range from famous athletes and celebrities in the entertainment world, to business men and factory workers.

These examples may provide a clue for us as we attempt to understand the process of "living through" a stuck-place in life. Part of the answer seems to be a matter of the heart more than the head. Thinking about a desperate situation often intensifies our confusion and frustration. Allowing our hearts to open through meditation or a caring relationship can awaken hope and enable us to "hang on" until the new possibility emerges.

I believe that once our hearts are touched by love, we make it possible to receive new ideas and inspiration for the future. I cannot explain this phenomenon; it is wrapped in mystery. But after many years of counseling men and women, I am convinced that the workings of the universe are essentially friendly to us.

Loving opens us to receive new gifts and blessings. Kubler-Ross discovered this. The man, whose inner voice told him to forgive himself, experienced it. And both found their lives changed in ways they describe as miraculous. The source of this mysterious concern for our welfare may be seen as the Holy Spirit, a Guardian Angel, a spiritual guide, or simply a beneficent universe. Naming it is less important than accepting it as a reality. Countless examples I have witnessed convince me of its genuineness.

The remarkable foundress of the Carmelite Order of nuns, St. Teresa of Avila, faced innumerable "stuck points" in her life. Often discouraged, she never lost hope that God would provide an answer, or indicate a new direction for her life. Her love for God, and her devotion to her nuns kept her heart open and receptive. And as proof of her maintenance of an inner spiritual balance, she never lost her sense of humor. During some of her greatest challenges she was able to bring a touch of laughter to a desperate-appearing situation.

This great woman, blessed with common sense and an infectious sense of humor, was able to view such situations *sub specie aeternitatis,* by the norms of eternal rather than temporal values. She trusted that God would provide for her as she was caring for His children. St. Teresa can serve as a role model for us, as we face our own difficult decisions and frightening "stuck places." Viewed from the perspective of a lifetime or eternity, desperation can be lessened and our hearts opened.

St. Teresa had a favorite saying that put reality into sharp focus for her. It is beautiful in its simplicity and its underlying message has brought me much strength and reassurance during difficult moments. It is a gift of peace for your soul. It is a saying that we all can use to restore balance to our priorities in life, and lift our hearts as we face the future. The saying is, **"This, too, shall pass."**

CHAPTER SIXTEEN

The Lilt of Laughter

Norman Cousins gave us a beautiful gift as his parting legacy—the value of laughter as a source of healing. His initial discovery, described in his book, *The Anatomy of An Illness,* came during a life-threatening illness as he watched movies of famous comedians. The laughter lessened his pain and relaxed his body so that he could have a few hours of restful sleep. Gradually he was able to stimulate the activity of his immune system and ultimately his health was restored. Afterwards, he became a veritable missionary of humor, teaching people all over the world about the healing power of laughter.

Cousins has aptly described laughter as "internal jogging." It serves as a mental and emotional form of aerobics, expanding our mental vistas, and breathing fresh air into our capacity for change. It can pull us out of the rut of fixed thinking as it breaks the bonds of inner tensions. Laughter has a kind of lilt that lightens heavy emotions and lifts our hearts. Who has not experienced the delight of being burdened by concerns, and then suddenly finding that a witty remark or a funny incident has caused laughter which brings a marvelous release of tension?

I have found that some of my best work in counseling has involved the use of laughter. There is a bit of the "ham actor" in me, and at times in a session I would role-play someone in the life of the client. I might overact outrageously, and the client and I would both end up laughing at me. For those few moments, tension was released, and some of the pain diminished. With lighter feelings we could move from overanalyzing the problem to searching for a solution.

Using fantasy or visualization has also helped to induce some moments of laughter. On one occasion I remember asking a young woman to imagine her boss in a new way. She found him intimidating, and was not able to confront or respond to him when he scolded her. She said, "He bedevils me." I asked her to picture him as a red devil, wearing funny red flannel sleepwear and carrying a pitchfork, while scolding her. After a few minutes she started to smile, then chuckle, and finally she laughed uproariously. The next week she reported that the fantasy served her well, since she was able to smile as he scolded her, calling to mind her image from the fantasy. She added that she felt this was a powerful aid in overcoming other fears.

I gained more understanding of the lilting effect of laughter during an evening I spent with a group of a dozen men and women. This was a support group for people in remission from cancer. I had been asked to give a talk to them, but fortunately my intuition suggested something else. After introducing myself, I said, "Rather than giving a talk this evening, I would like to offer you an invitation to join me in entertaining one another with amusing stories from our lives. Hopefully we will enjoy the stories and we may even experience the healing effect of laughter."

I began with a couple of incidents from my own life, and gradually as the laughter grew everyone was eager to share a humorous experience from the past. We laughed until tears flowed, and at the end of the evening we shared our feelings of lightness and closeness to each other. In the ensuing weeks I heard from several members of the group, who told me that not only was the evening enjoyable, but that it served as an important reminder of the power of laughter as a healing agent

Another learning from that evening was the realization that many of the amusing incidents recalled were embarrassing moments from the past. And I remember that similar sharing in encounter groups had the same effect of producing a closeness that seemed to be based on the common bond of our humanness. We may admire great deeds, but we can more readily identify with others who do "dumb" things or make fools of themselves. I had an opportunity to prove this when I was lecturing to counselors in Japan. I found that humor is often difficult to translate. So rather than attempt to lighten the talk with western-style humor, I decided to tell stories of my experiences as a bumbling "gaijin" or foreigner.

My first blunder occurred at the home of friends where I was staying. My host prepared the furo, or hot bath, for me. I had a wonderful warm soak, washed my body, and drained and cleaned the tub. The next day my host very kindly informed me that in Japan, the bath was for soaking. Washing took place on a small stool outside the tub, and after several washings, then the soak took place. I felt like a fool, especially when I realized that I had cheated my friend and his wife of a good hot bath because I had used all the water. The story brought chuckles to my Japanese audiences who had similarly embarrassing experiences with bathing western-style in hotels.

Another story which consistently brought laughter to my Japanese friends was a description of my first embarrassing experience with a Japanese-style toilet. These experiences reveal the fact that people everywhere can appreciate the embarrassment of human errors and ignorance, and their laughter shows their sense of identification with the one embarrassed.

It seems to me that most of us are starved for the food of laughter. We often build walls of protections around us, but these may be keeping out the life-giving nourishment of laughter. And that explains why we so appreciate a dear friend who can make us laugh with a witty remark or a funny story. At times, it may even be the key factor in survival. A friend has told me that on two separate occasions his life was saved by people who were able to bring a moment of laughter into his life while imprisoned at the death camp of Auschwitz. When tragedy strikes, we need such moments of lightness to counterbalance the pain and heartache.

My mother experienced such a gift when my niece died of cancer at a young age. Unable to attend the funeral because of a prior stroke, she was joined by a dear friend who possessed a marvelous Irish wit. As they sat together, they chatted about everything except the pain of my mother's loss. Finally this woman said to my mother, "Alice, do you know what we both need right now?" My mother said, "What?" Her friend said, "We both need a good cry." My mother, already beginning to weep, said through her tears, "But I don't want to cry!"

And the humor of her remark touched her and brought laughter out of the tears. My mother, after this release, and fortified with a glass of wine, could talk about her grandchild and allow some inner healing to take place. She later remarked that her friend, with her gift for laughter, had indeed been a godsend to her.

It is surprising how much even a small bit of humor can lighten our spirit and provide a slightly different perspective. I have always admired men and women who can think of a clever response to a situation. I smile as I remember Ronald Reagan, just after the assassination attempt, being asked how he felt as he was being wheeled into the hospital. He responded, quoting W.C. Fields, "Well, all things considered, I'd rather be in Philadelphia." His remark eased the tension for everyone. And there is the example of Phyllis Diller using humor to explain the cast on a broken arm, as she appeared on stage for a night club performance. She said, "For anyone who has just bought the book, *The Joy of Sex,* there is a misprint on page 206."

Pope John XXIII was also a man gifted with a lively wit. One of my favorite stories about his sense of humor describes a time he was walking with a man in the Vatican Gardens. The man asked him how many men were working in the gardens. With a twinkle in his eye, the pontiff replied, "About half of them."

And even though I do not consider myself to have a very quick wit, I do recall one time when I surprised myself. In the recovery room after I had an operation for pneumonia, a young nurse about to insert the needle for intravenous feeding said to me, "Dr. Auw, you probably don't remember me but I was one of your students in college." I turned, groggily, to look at her and said, "No, I don't remember you, but I hope I gave you a good grade." Yes, you gave me an A." "Wonderful," I replied, "proceed with the I. V.!"

The incident also illustrates the value of laughter in a hospital. I recall Bernie Siegel describing a humorous moment that occurred while he was operating on a patient to remove a cancerous tumor. He said that he liked to have music piped into the room during an operation, and found it soothing for himself and the patient. In this case, it was a song by Frank Sinatra, and the patient as well as the hospital personnel laughed at the appropriateness of the lyrics, "All of me, why not take all of me."

A bit of laughter can also work wonders in breaking the tension of boredom. A famous story tells of a dinner, honoring Marconi, given to celebrate the twenty-fifth anniversary of the invention of radio. The speeches were long and tiresome with fulsome praise for the inventor. But the last man to speak got a standing ovation for his brief remarks that brought laughter to the assembled group. He said, "We honor Mr. Marconi, and rightly so, for this marvelous gift of radio, but at the same time there may be a man who in some ways is even more important." Then he added, "And that is the man who invented the button that turns the damn thing off." Even Marconi roared with laughter and joined in the applause.

The release that comes with laughter may be only momentary, but it should not be underestimated. Research indicates that these brief interruptions of our tension and stress permit the body to send a form of healing energy to build the immune system and defend against illness. This is a truth that has been accepted, even though not scientifically demonstrated, by healers and spiritual teachers throughout the Far East for centuries.

Pir Vilayat, the Sufi teacher, has said that we should judge a guru by how much laughter is a part of his life. And Alan Watts, one of the pioneers in bridging Eastern and Western spirituality, taught that it is good for us to act silly enough to make us laugh at ourselves, and he had no use for gurus who paraded their holiness before the world. He dismissed them by saying, "I would never trust a saint who wasn't a little bit naughty."

One of my own healers is a man who knows the value of laughter. He is a chiropractor whom I visit occasionally for a pinched nerve in my shoulder. As he is working on me, we exchange amusing stories. And while I am in the midst of a humorous vignette, he makes the adjustment that releases the muscle spasm, and then we both have a good laugh. I tell him, "You tricked me again! I was so involved with my story that I forgot to tense-up, as I am inclined to do." And if all else fails, he has a silly cartoon-like smiling face pasted on the ceiling above his recline board that invariably makes me chuckle when I see it, and in that moment the bodily healing begins.

Laughter can bring fresh air to the mind and heart, toning for the body, and nourishment for the soul. We come to see things anew, experience ourselves differently, and judge priorities with a kinder measuring rod. Laughter, more swiftly than anything else, creates a better balance in our lives, and touches us with delight and joy. It does not solve our problems, or overcome our obstacles, or banish all our fears. It does something even better.

Laughter, the lilting gift of God, enables us to stand tall in the midst of our ills, and smile at the "cosmic joke," knowing that we have the secret of keeping our balance and of ultimately prevailing.

CHAPTER SEVENTEEN

Traveling Light

Many years ago I took a trip to England. An inexperienced traveler, I chose a two-suiter and a companion piece of luggage for the trip. I also packed enough clothes for a stay of several seasons. I managed, with a fair bit of struggle, to haul my luggage up the stairs of a small hotel in London, all the while muttering about the weight of my combined traveling cases.

However, the great awakening came when I decided to travel to Holland via the boat-train from Harwich. Upon arrival at Victoria Station, I found out that I would have to carry my luggage for several blocks in order to arrive at my designated train. Finally I boarded the train, found my seat and then collapsed. By this time I was drenched in perspiration, suffering from an aching back and untold strained muscles, as the dawning moment came to me. Like Poe's raven, I heard myself uttering a similar vow: Never again!

Since then, I have learned to pare down my list of necessary items to the point where I am able to pack for a month's visit with a single small suitcase, often a carry-on. I have become quite adept at making one outfit serve several purposes, and do not mind washing out a few articles of clothing along the way.

I was heartened to find a kindred spirit in Ann Barry, who wrote in *At Home in France* of her good fortune to find a companion with similar feelings about traveling light. She writes: "We also agree on the critical matter of baggage: one piece of luggage is the limit. That means reappearing in the same outfit, but who cares?"

I also realized at some point that my life had followed a similar pattern. I have moved about every ten years, and with each move I disposed of some of my possessions. Books have been shared with others, rather than filling a shelf. The same is true for records and tapes that I rarely listen to any more. And once a year, at Thanksgiving time, I clean out my closets and cupboards to donate articles that will be given to people at Christmas by a local charitable organization. I feel better with fewer possessions. I am also pleased that others will be able to enjoy these things.

I was reminded of this recently when I attended the memorial service for a dear friend. At the conclusion of the service, the minister announced that this woman requested that her large collection of books and tapes be made available after the service for those attending, and the balance be given to the church library. It was a thoughtful and generous gift, and also served as a reminder of the relative value of material things.

It seems to me that most of us go through life with too much baggage. We tend to accumulate things—material possessions—many of which we no longer need. Some of us have what is termed a "depression mentality." This refers to people who were raised during the years of the Great Depression in the 1930's, when it was necessary to scrimp and save in order to merely exist. Parents taught their children not to waste food, and to save items that later might be put to use.

I had such a friend. In her basement she had stored boxes of old clothes, pieces of material, even used ribbons and wrapping paper. Unfortunately she found years later that the clothes were moth-eaten, the pieces of material were not usable for anything but rags, and the wrapping paper was too wrinkled to be serviceable. Yet only when she had to move into an apartment was she able to give these things away or consign them to the refuse heap.

The real problem here is with one's attitude. People who cannot part with their possessions have an inner sense that they need these things. But in reality, most often they find that it is a false sense, a kind of hidden belief that having things will give them security or bring them happiness.

In reading the biography of Humphrey Bogart, I recall a statement made by him shortly before his death. He told Alistair Cooke that having money, a Jaguar, a great house and a boat, which once gave him great pleasure, were no longer of any comfort to him when he was so ill. At that point he was able to release his attachment to these things because he no longer needed them. This attitude is underlined by a famous remark of De Rance, the great cleric whose writing helped reform religious orders in the nineteenth century. He said, "It is not the man who has much who is rich, but the man who needs little."

Traveling light, then, is mostly determined by our attitudes. And among these, perhaps the most powerful are those which are concerned with our inner life, our emotions and emotional experiences.

As a counselor, I have listened to many stories of the pain caused by the burden of emotional baggage, as well as the problems resulting from the weight of demands that we place upon ourselves. I think of women who struggle to "have it all," attempting to juggle roles of a career with those of wife and mother, and experiencing frustration and exhaustion. Or of men, who find that their job leaves little time for family and relaxation. These may be the result of unrealistic goals or expectations which are "impossible dreams."

Many of these attitudes may arise from guilt over the past or fear for the future, and can become almost unbearable burdens that we carry throughout our adult lives. Yet, despite the pain of these emotional burdens, many find it even more difficult to let go of them than it is to discard unneeded material possessions. And with some who harbor feelings of hurt, the desire for revenge makes them prisoners of their own pain.

A friend in Paris illustrated this for me. He told of a reunion with men and women who had been in prison camps in World War II. He described his surprise and sadness at discovering the continuing hatred and bitterness of these people fifty years after the event. He said,

> *"I realized that although we had been freed from the prison camp, many were still in a prison fashioned from their desire for revenge. Their hearts were hardened and their lives were miserable."*

Such clinging to these poisonous attitudes is indeed sad, and often only a dramatic life event can create the conditions for a change that can lead toward inner freedom.

A successful executive told me recently of learning the lesson of traveling light—the hard way. He said,

> *"I had a quadruple bypass heart operation that scared me. The stress of managing a large firm, along with a great need to excel at everything, brought on the heart attack. I realized that I could continue my old pattern and die as a result, or I could adopt more realistic goals. I started to 'unload.' I learned to delegate responsibilities. I paced myself according to my level of energy, even taking a brief nap in the afternoon.*
>
> *Guess what? The company ran more smoothly, morale improved, and I found my employees going out of their way to make this transition easier for me. Not surprisingly, my wife and children responded with more affection and concern, which touched me deeply. Life is so much better for us, since I have learned a new set of values, and have discarded my old expectations."*

It has often struck me that we tend to overlook the pattern of nature as a lesson in the wonderful balance existing in the universe. Nature has seasons consisting of wonderful changes. And these are preceded by a process of shedding. Trees shed leaves in autumn, blossoms in spring, and fruit in summer. There is a special beauty to each aspect of the process. Animals shed their heavy coats of fur and creatures of the sea shed their shells when they outgrow them. **Nature tells us that shedding is the prelude to rebirth, both necessary and desirable.** Only humans have the ability to allow their fears to question this process. Perhaps it is time to listen to nature as a loving teacher to guide us as we face our own changes in life.

There is also a spiritual dimension to this concept of traveling light. In early Christian tradition, the apostles and missionaries were instructed to be concerned only with their daily needs, their "daily bread." They were to resist the temptation to become attached to things as well as places.

Thus the "spirit of poverty" was viewed more as a trust in the providence of a loving God, than in the issue of having or not having material goods. It was an attitude that enabled them to focus on the needs of others, believing that the God who cared for the birds of the air and the lilies of the field would supply their basic needs.

For them traveling light meant having this vital faith and hope, which freed them from worries and fears over material things. It gave them also a lightness of spirit that aided them in letting go of the past, and opening their hearts to the inner hurts of men and women they would meet, and to whom they would offer compassion.

Their lives might well serve as an inspiration for us. One of our greatest challenges in life is that of learning how to free ourselves of burdens. We carry the heavy weight of past hurts and woundings from childhood, as well as our adult relationships. In counseling, many men and women reveal the pain of remembered outrage which continues to leave a bitter taste in their hearts. What a joy it can be to discover that we can learn ways of letting go of these past burdens. Our hearts can once again sing and dance when liberated of the burden of hatred and resentment.

One of the paths to inner freedom is that of forgiveness. To offer our forgiveness to someone who has hurt us, is to enable us to unload the weight of resentment and bitterness we have been carrying. Unfortunately many people misunderstand forgiveness as a kind of weakness, or white washing, of the person concerned. It is nothing of the kind.

Forgiveness does not suggest that the actions of the perpetrator are condoned. Rather, genuine forgiveness recognizes the action, admits the hurt, understands the responsibility involved, and then chooses to offer the gift of forgiveness to that person. Essentially, forgiveness is not FOR that person.

Forgiveness is for us, enabling us to relieve ourselves of a burden we have held for too long. It is the gift of freedom that we give ourselves, in order to lighten our spirit and allow us to move on in life, attending to the cares and concerns of others. We may need help to adopt an attitude of forgiveness, but it is reassuring to know that developing such an attitude is within our reach and available to all of us.

I also recall a young woman whose mother had been abandoned as an infant, and whose entire adult life was colored by bitter resentment towards the mother that deserted her. Her daughter realized at one point that she had unconsciously adopted similar feelings, and her life was marked by an inability to trust, and to open her heart to others. At first she harbored resentment towards her mother for these feelings, but that soon changed.

During a workshop, the group was instructed to examine people in the past who had hurt each of them, and then to offer those persons a genuine gift of forgiveness. The young woman was able to do this toward several people from her past, but especially towards her mother. She told of her feelings when she returned home from the workshop,

> *"I could not believe how free I felt. All of the pain from the past was gone. No more anger or bitterness. I felt suffused by warmth, and filled with love, almost lighthearted and joyful. It was a type of rebirth for me, and one that I would have thought impossible."*

An interesting corollary to the experience of unburdening is the fact that not only do these men and women delight in feelings of being free, they tend to be more sensitive to the needs of others. They begin to care about and want to reach out to others. And in so doing, they are demonstrating the true nature of the gift of freedom. We tend to think of freedom in terms of what we are freed from. But this is only one aspect of the gift. The ultimate purpose of the gift is to enable us to be free for a higher and nobler end. Freedom is intended to open our hearts to love others.

And this, finally, is what gives meaning to life: the ability to love and to be loved. It is possible only when we have emptied our hearts of the dark energy of hatred and resentment, discarded the attachment to old fears, and replaced these with the life-giving energy of love. Thus free, we can begin to fulfill our personal life mission.

The invitation to a more fulfilling life is always extended to us. The pathway is learning to travel light. Eastern philosophers call this "the way of detachment," of unloading needless baggage, and unhooking ourselves from purely self-serving attachments, whether these be to material things, to people, or to attitudes. **Freedom is the reward of traveling light.**

St. Paul reminds us of the invitation which arrives with the gift of freedom. He writes, "You should be free to serve one another in love." (Gal:4,13)

CHAPTER EIGHTEEN

Responsible Response

The scene is the living room of my sister. Neighbors are enjoying a drink with us before dinner, when a boy approaches the neighbor couple and addresses his remarks to the husband. He is my sister's grandson, about nine years old. Standing before the man he says, "I'm sorry, but I lost your bicycle lock and chain. When I went to the store I left the chain unlocked and it was stolen, but I bought another one and hope it is O.K." He had been given use of the bike during his visit.

The neighbor re-assured the boy that all was well, hugged him and thanked him for his honesty. I was touched by the simple act of the boy's accepting responsibility for an error in judgement, for correcting the error, and for his courage in admitting it.

The incident had special significance because this took place just after the infamous Watergate scandal, when top officials of our government, including our President, were lying about involvement and seeking to cover up, to hide, and to blame others.

It is not only refreshing, but also inspiring to discover reminders that honesty and integrity are still valued and practiced. I have a friend who told me that his model of honesty during his childhood years was an older sister. He said, "I never knew her to tell a lie. Many times it would have meant avoiding a punishment, but she refused to lie, and I have thought of her example many times when tempted to avoid the truth."

I believe we all have heroes who have inspired us by accepting responsibility for their actions and bravely meeting difficult challenges. One of mine was an algebra teacher I had as a freshman in an all-male Jesuit high school. His introductory talk described the wonders we would be able to perform at the end of the school year, and almost as an aside he concluded by saying, "I will grade you fairly, but you also need to know I will not tolerate cheating. It is beneath one's dignity to cheat." At the end of the first week, he gave us a test for which most were unprepared. He asked us to pass the papers to the boy behind us, with instruction to correct the papers as he read the answers. Well, we sought to help one another out by changing some of the answers in order to improve slightly our dismal scores.

The papers were turned in and Mr. Procter started to read our scores. We were seated in alphabetical order, and the reading was an experience in shame that I still recall. The room became utterly silent as he read, "Mr. Acton, your score is zero. You cheated by changing figures two and four of your neighbor's paper. Mr. Baker, your score is zero. You changed three figures for your friend. Mr. Caldwell, your score…" By the time he got to the last student we were in a state of devastation. When he had finished he stood up and said, "Perhaps you didn't understand me when I said it the first time, so I will repeat it. Cheating is beneath one's dignity." With that he walked out of the room.

At our thirty-fifth high school reunion, I asked several of my former classmates if they remembered that incident. It was still vivid in their minds. "And did you ever cheat again on an exam?" Their responses were unanimous: "No!" The lesson, though painful, served as an ongoing reminder of the value of honesty and the important part it plays in the way we choose to live throughout our lives.

Honesty is a theme that recurs constantly in counseling. Many people carry heavy burdens of guilt over dishonest acts from the past. Small thefts, little lies, evidence of betraying a trust, can weigh heavily upon the soul. One man told of stealing a piece of gum from the purse of a woman visiting his mother. Forty years later he was still bothered by his inability to confess his misdeed to this woman whom he saw many times after the event. Had he chosen to do so, he most likely would have been rewarded by the woman for his honesty over this small matter, but even if she did not do so, he would have felt cleansed and forgiven because he had acted with integrity. Inner satisfaction is the reward of responsible action.

In fact, betrayal of trust seems to be judged with less severity than dishonesty. Many times a client will say, "The thing that hurt me the most is that my husband (wife) lied to me when confronted about the affair." This seems true even in scandals involving persons in positions of authority. Some years ago, the Profumo Affair in England involved a high government official and a Russian spy who were sharing the affections of a prostitute. When accused, Mr. Profumo denied any sort of involvement with the woman. Later when it was clear that he had lied, he was forced to resign and his career was ruined. One commentator said,

"The British people can understand a man's dalliance, but they can never forgive his lying to the public. Had he said that he had sinned, was sorry and asked to be forgiven, he would probably be in office today."

Fear most often is the reason for our failure to act responsibly. Fear fuels our feelings of insecurity and encourages us to avoid doing the honorable thing. Overcoming these feelings is best learned in childhood, beginning with small tasks and simple instructions to do what needs to be done. The child learns that there is a right way and a wrong way to behave, and that consequences follow our actions.

The child begins to develop a moral or ethical sense when the parent does more than make demands. Sometimes the child needs help in overcoming the fear of not being able to please the parent, or help in being encouraged to do the right thing. This support can enable the child to choose sacrifice. He can then discover the internal reward of having acted honorably and generously. Later this learning will facilitate more difficult choices in adolescent and adult life.

A client described an incident from his childhood that made an impact on his entire adult life. In the first grade of a Catholic grammar school he joined his fellow students in sacrificing some of the candy money for a collection to feed orphan children overseas. One day, after he had donated ten cents, the teacher counted the coins and announced that they were short of their goal by five cents. The boy had a nickel left in his pocket, and he intended to buy a candy bar a lunchtime.

No one else offered to complete the fund and the boy struggled with himself for several minutes. Finally, he made the choice, walked up to the teacher's desk and deposited his five cents in the collection box, to the applause of the students and teacher. As an adult remembering this event he said,

> *"It was the best investment I ever made. Many times since then I have been tempted to hold back, to be selfish rather than generous, and each time I recall that first grade experience, I choose to be generous. I have never regretted those choices. In fact, I am sure I have given a good example to others."*

Over the years I have learned to trust my own intuition in guiding me to make responsible responses. One incident stands out as an example. I had been invited to take part in a training program for Japanese executives. The program was conducted in Japanese, so my understanding of the training process was very limited. However, I learned to listen to the tone of the voice and body language and had a fair sense of what the men were experiencing.

At one point, after a Gestalt exercise in which one of the men engaged in a role-play involving his father, he sat on the floor and wept, with his face in his hands. Somehow I seemed to understand his anguish and, not wondering whether it would be appropriate or not, I followed my heart. I sat down on the floor behind the man, and put my arms around him. He turned and leaned against my chest as he sobbed out some of his pain in words that I could not translate. Yet, I knew that he was talking to his father through me.

It was a moment of great emotion for all of us and later the man thanked me for enabling him to bring closure to a very troubled and guilt-ridden relationship with his father. The incident also served as a reminder for me that these intuitive responses were indeed ways of enabling me to do the right thing at a given moment.

I have also learned that spontaneous responses are not always responsible ones. An emotional reaction can provoke a response that we may later regret. Angry or critical remarks when we feel attacked may not be responsible reactions. How then can we tell when a proposed response is appropriate to the situation? One of the best ways to determine this is to ask ourselves, "What am I responding to?"

If the answer is fear or anger or a desire to seek revenge, then most likely we are not acting in our own best interests, not acting responsibly. If the answer is a desire to offer help, communicate caring, give a gift to another person, or simply to express some inner joy, then the chances are that our action will be a responsible one.

In essence, a responsible response at its highest expression comes from recognizing a genuine human need and acting to meet that need. The heart is touched and the hands reach out to offer aid and support. A wonderful example occurred recently in Hawaii when a three year old girl needed a bone marrow transplant. An article was written in the paper, along with pictures of the child and her young parents. The accompanying story told of the difficult search for matching bone marrow. Within a few months over thirty thousand people volunteered to be tested.

Ultimately, a match was found and the child survived the delicate operation. The response of generous men and women gave new life and inspiration to an entire community.

Responsible response is a choice that arises from our finest inner gifts of honesty and integrity. And, like the Biblical promise of a gift in return for "bread cast upon the waters," we receive an increase in strength of character, along with inner satisfaction and quiet joy.

CHAPTER NINETEEN

Learning to Learn

In reading Katherine Graham's autobiography, I became aware that the book was more than a story of her life. It was an articulate description of her growth as a woman. From a childhood and youth filled with insecurities, she developed into a person of strength and self-confidence. As publisher of *The Washington Post* newspaper she became a prominent figure in the media world and a powerful force in the political arena.

Her story, as she recalls past life events, is essentially one of education. She now views these experiences as a series of life-lessons, an ongoing learning process. Despite dramatic and tragic happenings, Kay Graham was able to search for and find ways to utilize these painful experiences for her own growth. She learned to turn mistakes into stepping-stones to new knowledge and wisdom. And at the same time, she deepened her compassion and understanding of human frailty.

This remarkable woman possessed one special gift that enabled and encouraged her to survive challenging situations and turn them to her own personal growth. That gift was an openness to learning. As a child and even as a young woman she lived with the belief that no one else was as stupid or foolish to make the kind of mistakes she did. Later, she came to realize that everyone makes mistakes, and that the importance of such an experience is to learn how to use mistakes for one's growth.

I believe this insight is one that marks the beginning of wisdom for a person. It lifts us above the petulant, blaming, whining behavior of a child and enables us to take responsibility for changing our behavior. Instead of merely crying and complaining, we are able to address the issue, even through our tears. Like Katharine Graham, we can then say, "O.K., I made a mistake. Now what can I learn from that and how can I correct what I have done?"

One of the challenges facing a counselor is that of helping clients to come to this insight. They arrive burdened by hurt, sometimes filled with resentment and anger. Often as they pour out their painful feelings to an understanding listener, they feel the need to assign blame for their current situation. The challenge facing them is to release these feelings and learn from the distressing experience. But blame can be a seductive siren. It can give us a temporary feeling of inner satisfaction, while keeping us prisoners of our resentment. Only when we are able to accept our experience as an opportunity to learn can we make the choice to take responsible action for our future life.

Recently, a young man told me of his sense of relief at being able to release years of resentment. He said,

> *"I have held a huge amount of anger in my heart toward my mother. I felt she had abandoned me, and deprived me of the love I needed as a child. It affected*

my whole life, and especially my marriage. But one day I realized that this anger was destroying me. With counseling I was able to move away from the past, to forgive my mother, and start giving more love to my wife and children. I had to learn to let go, learn to forgive and learn to focus on my present life, but the learning has given me my first taste of true happiness."

This is an example of the growth of a man out of childhood thinking, and into a perspective that contains the seeds of wisdom.

The learning process that leads to such changes in attitude and behavior seldom is a simple or easy one. It seems to me that advice, though well intentioned, rarely opens us to new learning. Most often we need a caring relationship, and a sense of shared trust before it becomes possible for us to open our hearts. The problem we experience is not one of information, but one of heart-wounding. We need to feel some healing in the heart before we can be willing to accept new ways of thinking and new choices in our lives. And I have found that once this supportive relationship is established, the healing and learning can be fostered best by an indirect approach.

Many times a seemingly unrelated experience will enable us to release our fixation with painful past events. A moment of shared laughter can effect a moment of release. For a brief period of time fear dissipates, and the tension of fear vanishes. Role-playing or the description of an embarrassing experience can sometimes lead to unexpected laughter and a lightness of feeling. From this moment of shared safety, we may be able to re-examine our need to hold on to anger over past hurts. We can then choose to learn a lesson from the past rather than give it ongoing life at great cost to our inner peace.

Maria Montessori discovered that children especially learn best when the learning is indirect. She found that play is the language of learning for children. If they engage in playful activity that is fun, they will be open to gaining a variety of lessons from the experience. Didactic instruction is much less effective, partly because children love to feel they have been a part of the discovery. It is like a treasure hunt where they find the hidden gold coins. As they have been a part of the adventurous search, the learning becomes their own reward, and part of them.

In a similar way, I have found that adults in counseling learn life lessons best when they have been a part of the search rather than having someone tell them what they should do to solve their problems. At times people simply need to discover new possibilities or options, which they cannot find by themselves while they are paralyzed with fear and blinded by anger or hurt.

I once said to a client, "If you could wave a magic wand and do anything that your heart desired, what would it be?" After first starting to object, I reminded her that a magic wand overcomes such obstacles. Finally she said, rather timidly, "Well, I would love to own a little shop selling clothes and artifacts from South America." We then engaged in a guided fantasy, buying interesting items from several countries and bringing them back to a small shop in Hawaii.

After the fantasy this woman smiled and said, "Oh, wouldn't that be great, *but* it is only a dream. I could never make it a reality." I replied, "Perhaps you cannot, but it is equally possible that perhaps you can." And then we began to examine possibilities. Out of this came a decision to interview a woman who had a successful business selling unusual items from Asia. Later, an ad in the University newspaper connected her with a woman who shared her dream. Together they were able to find some modest financing, and now have a small shop which is doing very well. The business has given them both a new sense of self-confidence and an appreciation of the importance of mutual support.

Networking with others, acquiring not only information, but also inspiration to take new risks, is a way of gaining additional alternatives. The learning process can then move us from feelings of impotency to a growing sense that we just might be able to make our dream come true.

The Montessori Method can also be characterized as "Learning by Doing." It implies experimentation, trying other ways to obtain a desired result, and often being surprised at learning lessons beyond the task at hand. Some of these are important, value-laden life lessons. This indirect learning can be seen when someone reaches out to help others. The focus upon one's own pain is exchanged for a compassionate feeling towards the person being aided.

Hospital volunteers often report that an afternoon spent with seriously ill patients can have profound effects. They find themselves being creative in offering love and comfort, and feel good about that. In addition, their own pain seems less demanding and many express gratitude for the health they have, seeing their lives in a new perspective.

Dr. Bernie Siegel has described the impact of children with terminal cancer upon volunteer helpers. These men and women expected to bring comfort and cheer to dying children. What they discovered is that the children became their teachers. Through them they learned to bear pain, to be self-sacrificing, and even to face death without fear. They came to realize that the lessons of the heart are the most valuable of all life lessons.

I believe that there are rich sources of inspiration all around us which when tapped become ways of opening our hearts to deeper values. Nature is a veritable treasure house of gifts for us. The sight of a bird soaring in the sky, the wonder of clouds drifting through the blue heavens, the glory of a sunset at the edge of a rippling sea, the shadows upon hills of green in late afternoon. These scenes of natural beauty can touch the soul and open the heart to new meaning and learning for our current lives.

Some years ago I lived in a small cottage near the sea in La Jolla, California. I would often ask a client to take a "nature walk" with me. We would spend a few moments watching pelicans fishing, or marveling at the grace of whales playing with their pups not far offshore. Then we would stroll through winding streets admiring the beautiful flower gardens of residents. More than once a client would stop and examine a flower or bush that brought back happy childhood memories.

One man asked the name of a flower. It was a delphinium. He said, "My mother raised those and I used to help her weed that part of the garden. It was a special time for us." And a woman saw a sterling silver rosebush and said, "I had never seen a lavender colored rose before. I bought a rosebush and gave it to my godmother who valued it as her most prized possession and tended it with loving care until she died. I miss her and the love she lavished on me." These experiences with the beauty of nature can touch our souls, and open our hearts to new learning, inspiring us to share the love within us more generously with others.

I remember a man in Japan who had a similar experience and was moved to reach out to young students. A widower, he decided to invest his small bit of savings in a coffee shop. Unfortunately, the only rent he could afford was on the third floor of a building near the train station in his small town. Friends said he was fool to expect customers to climb to the third floor for cup of coffee. But he trusted his intuition, rented the area and opened his coffee shop.

At first he had few customers, mostly high school and college students who came because the coffee was cheaper at his cafe, and he had music and books available. Soon, young people began to meet there, and then he had an inspiration. He put out writing tablets and invited the students to jot down impressions, reflections, poems that had meaning for them.

The idea caught fire and before long students were also sharing not only reflections, but personal concerns and problems. Since these were all anonymous, there was a great spirit of openness. Other students would respond to some of the sharings, describing their own experiences and at times offering suggestions for solving problems that had been effective for them. Within a few months, the cafe was doing a wonderful business and making money for the owner.

Later, when I visited the cafe, the owner said to me, "This has given me a new life. These students are the children I never had. They come and tell me their problems, they thank me for giving them this chance to share with other young people and learn from one another. I see now that it is a kind of learning laboratory. The students learn from each other, they learn from me, and above all, I am able to learn from them. What a gift this has been for me."

And I echo his remark. What a gift! It is an eloquent story to illustrate the point that as we go out of ourselves, and reach out to others, we gain the gift of new learning and inspiration. The heart opens, the head follows, and the inner eye sees new realities, which in turn offer us new hope. Indeed, the prayer of St. Francis is literally true:
"It is in giving that we receive."

CHAPTER TWENTY

And Suddenly... A Butterfly

One of the most rewarding experiences for a counselor is being able to participate in those rare but magical moments of transformation. The process is often so gradual that both the client and the counselor are, in the words of C.S. Lewis, "surprised by joy" when the metamorphosis occurs. This is not merely a change in perception, or new intellectual insight. It is a radical shift in consciousness that touches the heart and soul, as well as the mind. It is a kind of new birth as a person, with new values and beliefs, and especially a sense of inner power.

The experience is similar to the incredible miracle of nature when a catepillar transforms into a butterfly. The movement of a person from despair to hope, from a meaningless existence to a life of dedication and service, these are dramatic forms of essential inner change and reasons for rejoicing. One of the pathways to this change is the discovery of our hidden potential. Counseling can help to illumine inner gifts and beauty, and to draw us to the search for other inner resources.

I remember a young woman who had difficulty in talking about her personal life, but she could draw a picture and use the distance of the drawing to discuss her concerns. The process of her drawings became a kind of metaphor in themselves. At first she used pen and ink, then colored crayons, then watercolors, and finally oils. The quality of the artwork changed. Her self-portraits became clearer and lovelier, as she discovered her ability to switch from a focus on her painful past history to "painting a more beautiful future." She also became aware of a sensitive eye for beauty, and came to accept the fact that this was a reflection of an inner beauty she had long denied.

This initial experience of her inner self grew and soon she found that she could look back upon her past with gentleness instead of fury, and compassion instead of blame. Most importantly, she found a new career as an artist. Few people today would guess that this warm, outgoing woman was once a recluse, afraid to meet strangers, and encircled by fear and anger.

Over the years I have been privileged to witness many transformations that have been equally impressive. And I have reflected on this phenomenon. I am saddened to realize that all too often the "butterfly person" in each of us remains deeply hidden. Even counseling often fails to reveal it. There is a tendency to focus upon problems with roots in the past. And while this can be helpful, it often leaves the client stuck in the problem.

I tend to agree with the belief that we do not solve a problem "at the level of the problem." The underlying level, the impact of the problem on the person, is the place that we need to work on. Thus, great therapists like Rogers and Satir were primarily concerned with empowerment—helping clients to discover inner resources, strength and self-confidence. Energized, the client could begin to seek alternate ways of resolving the problem.

Some years into my counseling practice, I began to search for more creative ways to lift the veil of the butterfly person that I glimpsed, but which remained hidden to the client. Role-playing, dreamwork, relaxation exercises, artwork, music, and dance were some of the ways that enabled the client to feel freer, less fearful, to experience release and the enjoyment of laughter. Gradually the beautiful person began to emerge from the imprisonment of the cocoon. I also discovered more of my own inner resources and beauty as we shared these growthful experiences.

In fact, the symbol of the butterfly has had great personal meaning for me. As a child, I witnessed the mysterious transformation of a caterpillar into this glorious creation with its delicate wings and beautiful colorings. Later I became fascinated with a collection of butterflies gathered by a young friend and his family on a trip to Borneo. And I was thrilled by the sight of thousands of Monarch butterflies gathered at a famous spot near Monterey, California.

I seemed to find references to butterflies at every turn. I read stories of the inmates of concentration camps in Europe drawing butterflies as decorations for their flimsy partitions. I heard Elisabeth Kubler-Ross describe children with terminal cancer choosing the butterfly as their favorite symbol. I found the butterfly featured in art and ceramic work in Japan and Thailand. In so many different cultures, the symbolism was the same.

The butterfly stood for metamorphosis, death and resurrection, the triumph of light over the forces of darkness, and the transformation from ugliness into beauty, from earthbound creatures into winged wonders able to soar in the heavens.

The curious aspect of this universal archetype is the fact that the butterfly represents not only a transformation. It symbolizes a triumph of transfiguration over the inner forces of evil and darkness. It expresses the secret yearnings of the human heart for ultimate fulfillment. The butterfly seems to remind us of a truth that has been hidden from us for too long: that there is a part of us blessed with an incredible inner beauty and power. It is almost as if this were an ancient universal consciousness which we are just beginning to find available to us.

Within this consciousness is the realization of a vast storehouse of talents and gifts, which have been our heritage forever and which we can now utilize. These represent treasure beyond our wildest dreams, or more accurately, the reality underneath our fondest imaginings. And therein lies another key to the mystery of lifting the veil which hides this truth from us—our imaginings.

As a child I discovered the treasure contained in our neighborhood library. I became a voracious reader. I soon outgrew the children's section, and found biographies, travel books, and ancient legends like the Arthurian tales to delight me, as well as to stir my imagination. I had a fantasy of reading all the books in the library and becoming learned and wise. And although I did not fulfill that fantasy, the sense of the library as a great treasury of information and inspiration remained with me.

I now see the library as a metaphor for the human person. There is such an abundance of riches within each of us, so much more than we immediately recognize. And when we can begin to sense some of our inner greatness we start the process of transformation into the "butterfly person" we have been called to become.

What is needed is permission to allow our imagination to express itself without restriction. The kind of imaginative soaring we experienced as children, traveling in our minds to distant ports of call, and ancient civilizations. Transcending space and time is the province of the imagination and it is the magic key to the castle of our inner riches.

Often during a counseling session I would ask the client to close his eyes, do a few breathing exercises to relax completely and then suggest a scene for him to picture. I would ask him to imagine himself back in the middle ages, living in his favorite castle. And when he could picture this, I would ask him to take me on a tour of the castle, describing its rooms and treasures, and the things that made this such a special place for him. As the tour progressed, the client would become more resourceful in discovering things of beauty and meaning. He saw himself as the proud possessor of objects of art and treasures from distant lands. And when it was time to end the tour, it was often with a touch of sadness that he said farewell to this special place.

In reflecting on the meaning of the fantasy, the client would discover a number of connections with his own life. He would uncover values hidden from childhood, dreams of greatness long repressed, and talents too long unused. Yet the awareness did not dampen his spirit, but stimulated and encouraged him to actualize more of his potential.

One young man found that he had placed a musical instrument in all of the major rooms of his castle, and recognized that he had denied his need for the nourishment of music, and decided to honor it. He has since attended concerts and operas and is now able to play the piano. Today he says, "I'm making up for lost time. Music is a part of me and has changed my life." The butterfly person is emerging, beginning with a flight of fantasy, and the lifting of an inner veil. But the most important point of this example is that what took place was not merely the development of a talent. It was a metamorphosis of a person, formerly locked in his own self-image as a man with little talent and few social skills, who had accepted his lot in life and dared not dream of moving beyond the poverty of his existence. This is the wonder that can come from the liberation of the imagination, and which for me as a counselor, is so rewarding: to see more than a solution to a problem. It is the joy of assisting at the birth a new person.

Realizing the power of imagination to effect transformation, it is puzzling to understand the general devaluation of this inner gift. Rationality has held the place of honor in our culture, and imagination was relegated to the position of an interesting source of entertainment, but more of a distraction than a valued part of our personality.

As children we may even have been scolded for our imaginings or daydreaming. In any event, we have been impoverished and handicapped by this bias. Today we have to learn a new way of perceiving ourselves, and this usually requires some kind of training. We have to exercise our mental muscles, stretching them in new ways to build strength and confidence in this new ability to utilize our imaginative powers.

Although specialized training with a professional who uses imaginative approaches is often helpful, we can still exercise these inner muscles by a variety of responses. While listening to instrumental music, we can close our eyes and allow our mind to picture scenes or experiences that arise. Reading a novel set in an earlier period can offer us a chance to imagine ourselves in that place and time, living a lifestyle very different from our present one. Watching floating clouds can encourage us to imagine formations that suggest faces or objects familiar to us, and even allow us to imagine riding on those clouds, as if on a magic carpet to an exciting new adventure.

These are simple ways in which we can see beyond the observable reality by also stimulating our creative abilities. Once activated, our imagination can be a source for new options and choices in life, and the initiator of healing for the body as well as the mind.

Today many physicians, such as Elisabeth Kubler-Ross, Carl Simonton, and Bernie Siegel, use fantasy as a means of activating a sluggish immune system in order to bring healing to people whose bodies have been weakened by illness and whose spirits have been devastated by fear and helplessness.

While in Tokyo, I treasure the visits with a dear friend who always nourishes my spirit. Now retired, for years she was Dean of Women at a famous university in Tokyo. Women sought her wise counsel and were inspired to dream of greatness and find the courage to allow the butterfly person within them to emerge. My visits with this charismatic woman remind me of the lessons she taught her students.

Metamorphosis is not merely for caterpillars, nor it is only the stuff of myths involving frogs, princes, and ugly ducklings. Encoded in our genetic material, just as truly as the color of our eyes or hair, is a call to greatness, an impulse to experience that part of us which lifts us above the mundane and touches upon the divine.

We need only to begin to believe, to dare to dream, to gently press against the imprisoning cocoon until one day...suddenly we are the butterfly person we have been destined to become.

Titles Published by Aslan

Argument With An Angel.
by Jan Cooper
$11.95
ISBN 0-944031-63-3

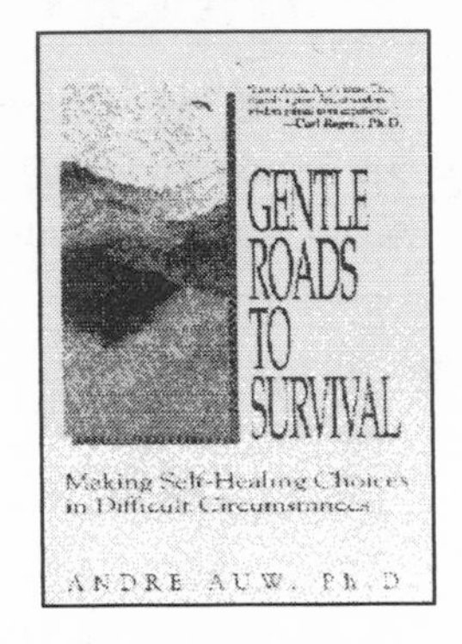

Gentle Roads To Survival: Making Self-Healing Choices in Difficult Circumstances
by Andre Auw Ph.D. $10.95
ISBN 0-944031-18-8

The Gift of Wounding: Finding Hope & Heart in Challenging Circumstances
by Andre Auw Ph.D.
$13.95
ISBN 0-944031-79-X

How Loving Couples Fight: 12 Essential Tools for Working Through the Hurt
by James L Creighton Ph.D.
$16.95
ISBN 0-944031-71-4

Intuition Workout: A Practical Guide To Discovering & Developing Your Inner Knowing
by Nancy Rosanoff
$12.95
ISBN 0-944031-14-5

The Joyful Child: A Sourcebook of Activities and Ideas for Releasing Children's Natural Joy
by Peggy Jenkins Ph.D.
$16.95
ISBN 0-944031-66-8

Lovers For Life: Creating Lasting Passion, Trust and True Partnership
by Daniel Ellenberg Ph.D. & Judith Bell M.S., MFCC
$15.95
ISBN 0-944031-61-7

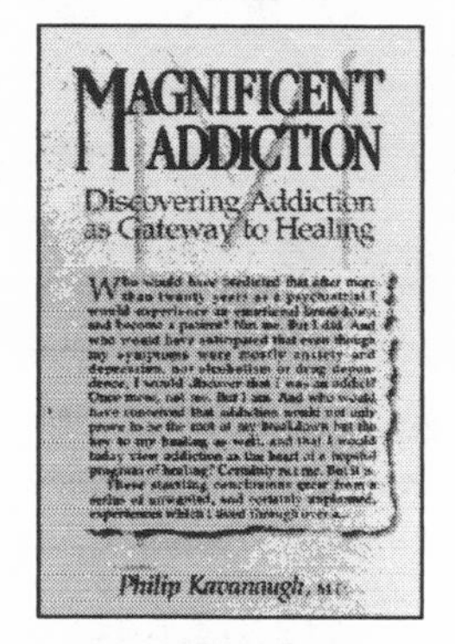

Magnificent Addiction: Discovering Addiction as Gateway to Healing by Philip R. Kavanaugh, M.D. $12.95
ISBN 0-944031-36-6

More Than Just Sex: A Committed Couples Guide to Keeping Relationships Lively, Intimate & Gratifying
by Daniel Beaver M.S., MFCC
$12.95
ISBN0-944031-35-8

Mind, Music & Imagery: Unlocking the Treasures of Your Mind
by Stephanie Merritt
$13.95
ISBN 0-944031-62-5

New Woman Manager: 50 Fast & Savvy Solutions for Executive Excellence
by Sharon Lamhut Willen
$14.95
ISBN 0-944031-11-0

The Motion Picture Prescription Watch This Movie and Call Me in The Morning: 200 Movies to help you heal life's problems by Gary Solomon Ph.D. "The Movie Doctor"
$12.95
ISBN 0-944031-27-7